BIRTH BY DEATH

Fedell Caffey took a pair of shears and started cutting Debra Evans's stomach open. He cut her abdomen crossways at first while Annette Williams watched. As he cut more, she could see the head of the baby sticking out. Caffey continued to cut the abdomen and the baby began to emerge. It was a boy.

It had no color and was covered with blood and mucus. Williams stood beside Caffey as he began to pull the baby completely out. It looked limp and she thought it was dead. Caffey cut the umbilical cord.

Williams grabbed the baby. She blew into his nose until he started coughing and breathing on his own. Dressing him in the hat and sleeper she had brought with her, she left the room.

She did not look back at the motionless body of her friend Debra, butchered and bloody on the floor.

Other books by Bill G. Cox

BORN BAD

OVER THE EDGE

SHOP OF HORRORS

NO SAFE PLACE

Published by Pinnacle Books

SPECIAL DELIVERY

BILL G. COX

PINNACLE BOOKS
Kensington Publishing Corp.

http://www.pinnaclebooks.com

Some names have been changed to protect the privacy of individuals connected to this story.

PINNACLE BOOKS are published by

Kensington Publishing Corp.
850 Third Avenue
New York, NY 10022

All Kensington Titles, Imprints, and Distributed Lines are available at special quantity discounts for bulk purchases for sales promotion, premiums, fund-raising, and educational or institutional use. Special book excerpts or customized printings can also be created to fit specific needs. For details, write or phone the office of the Kensington special sales manager: Kensington Publishing Corp., 850 Third Avenue, New York, NY 10022, attn: Special Sales Department, Phone: 1-800-221-2647.

Pinnacle and the P logo Reg. U.S. Pat. & TM Off.

First Printing: April 2001
10 9 8 7 6 5 4

Printed in the United States of America

This book is dedicated to my wife, Nina, the love of my life and my working partner, who helped so much with research, transcribing trial transcripts, and copyediting this book and the others we have done together.

ONE

Addison, Illinois, one of the western suburbs of Chicago, is a nice town that people looking for a good place to raise a family would pick to live in. The population is about 32,000—not too big, not too small.

Its nearness to Chicago, whose western city limits are less than ten miles away, might best be illustrated by an item in a book put together by Addison's centennial committee: back in the 1800s when the disastrous Chicago fire raged out of control, people in Addison could read a newspaper at night by the bright illumination from the big fire. Chicago at that time was eighteen miles away, said the local historians.

While its big-city neighbor has been plagued historically with criminal violence (the St. Valentine's Day Massacre involving seven murdered gang members in 1929, the sadistic murders of eight nurses by Richard Speck in 1966, the slaughter of thirty-four boys by John Wayne Gacy in the late 1970s), Addison is relatively free of violent crime.

It is a pleasant and friendly town with a strong economic base hinged on various industries. There are plenty of churches that are well attended. It has a sound town government and good schools, as well as resident families dating back several generations.

But on the night of Thursday, November 16, 1995, in an apartment complex on North Swift Road in west Addison, a little boy was caught up in a nightmare of unimaginable horror and terror that would make headlines worldwide.

The four burglars came through a window of the apartment. That is the way the seven-year-old boy later recalled it. He knew their names. They were friends of his mommy's.

But as he watched with sickening fear from his hiding place, they grabbed and cut and stabbed his mommy and his sister.

They killed them.

His mommy and sister lay on the floor, all bloody, not moving. He knew they were dead.

Sobs wracked his small body, but he hid from the mean people.

He waited until the burglars had left, until there was no sound except the TV still playing in the living room where his mommy was on the floor.

Then he grabbed his long green coat and jerked it on over the T-shirt and the underwear that he slept in. The sobbing boy didn't bother with his pants. He just pulled on his boots, and after another glance to make sure the burglars were gone, he ran into the kitchen, out the back door, and down the back stairs.

Too late the little boy saw that they were not gone.

One of the burglars grabbed him, hustled him into their car, and they drove away fast into the dark night.

The night was cold and getting colder.

James Edwards's shift had ended about 2:40 A.M. this Friday, November 17, 1995. He walked south down North Swift Road toward the apartment he shared with his longtime girlfriend, Debra Evans, and her three kids. He was glad it was just a two-minute walk from the factory where he worked the night shift.

As he neared the apartment building, Edwards was startled to see that all of the lights were on and the window blinds wide open in their apartment unit. Debbie and the kids should have been asleep long before this, blinds closed and lights off.

He entered the outside back door that he always kept ajar by inserting a folded rug so he would not have to walk all the way around the building to the front entrance.

He walked up the back stairway that led to a back hall and the inside back door of their apartment.

He inserted his key, tried to turn it, but discovered the door was unlocked. What in the devil was going on, he wondered. The door never was left unlocked this time of night.

He could hear the TV set blasting away inside their flat. When he pushed open the door, he was met by the youngest of Debbie's children, Jordan; the crying seventeen-month-old toddler was wearing his red sleeper.

Edwards picked up the youngster and began patting

and consoling him. Moving ahead with Jordan in his arms, Edwards noticed the kitchen was a mess—a cabinet drawer next to the sink pulled out, the utensil tray and other stuff scattered on the cabinet top.

In the living room he saw a hump underneath a Winnie-the-Pooh blanket on the floor between the love seat and coffee table. He thought it was Debbie playing some kind of game with him.

"Hey, come on, Debbie, what's going on?" Edwards said as he stooped to peel back the blanket covering her from head to foot.

Clad in gold-colored slacks and a gray sweater, the barefoot woman was faceup, her legs slightly spread. Blood was all over her face and throat and her pant legs and crotch area. Blood had spurted onto the love seat cushions and the floor.

His first thought was something had gone badly wrong with her pregnancy. The delivery time for her fourth child was close. Looking for the source of the massive bleeding, Edwards pulled up her sweater.

He reeled backward from the gruesome sight. Her stomach gaped wide open, slashed below the navel from one side to the other. Part of her insides were hanging out, dripping blood onto the carpet.

He grabbed the phone from the end table next to the love seat and dialed the 911 emergency number. The dialing panel was speckled with blood.

When the 911 operator answered, the frantic Edwards blurted excitedly, "I need an ambulance to—"

"Hold on, hold on, I'm gonna connect you," the operator interrupted.

"Oh man!" Edwards exclaimed.

The operator connected Edwards to the emergency fire dispatcher.

"Nine-one-one fire emergency," answered the dispatcher.

"Hey, could you send a hospital—could you send an ambulance here—!"

The dispatcher broke in. "What's the problem, sir?"

Edwards cried frantically, "My girlfriend is pregnant! I looked, and it's like her stomach is busted open! I just walked in the house! I don't know how long she's been here like this!"

The dispatcher was professionally calm, getting the address and the apartment number from the agitated caller.

"Okay, we'll be right there."

"Okay! Hurry, man!"

Edwards hung up.

The dispatcher at the Addison Police Department had started contacting patrol units to assist the ambulance service with the emergency call, repeating the address.

"Complications with a pregnancy," the dispatcher broadcast to a responding unit after the officer advised he was in the general area.

After hanging up, Edwards hurried to the small back bedroom where the two older children slept on separate futons on the floor. A light was on in the bedroom closet enabling him to see another blanket-draped figure on one of the sleeping pallets. Flipping down the cover, Edwards was stunned by the sight of ten-year-old Samantha Evans sprawled faceup, one arm flung out from her right side.

Oh God, she was killed like her mother. Blood

drenched the front of her Pocahontas nightgown, and he could see gaping, bloody holes in the side of her neck . . . blood on her face and legs and her right hand. Blood had soaked the pallet under her upper body. Her eyes were half open, but he knew she was dead.

Joshua, Samantha's seven-year-old brother, was nowhere in sight. His sleeping bag next to that of his sister was empty.

Edwards hollered the boy's name several times, receiving no response. With Jordan in his arms, he ran through the apartment and out the living room door and started pounding on the door of the apartment across the hall.

Bryan Hennessy opened the door. He was confronted by the hysterical James Edwards holding the toddler in his arms and babbling something about Debbie and Samantha were cut and bloody and dead.

For a few seconds Hennessy thought his neighbor was out of his head. Wide-eyed and almost incoherent, Edwards blurted, "What's been going on . . . what happened . . . oh man, did you hear them . . . see something, see anybody . . . will you come in there with me! I got to get some help!"

Hennessy's wife, Rebecca, appeared in a robe and took charge of Jordan as her husband went with Edwards.

Hennessy was shocked when he saw the body of Debbie Evans motionless on the floor, blood and vomit oozing from her mouth.

Going to the children's bedroom, the neighbor jerked

back with horror at the sight of the stabbed and slashed body of Samantha. He backed out of the room.

Edwards was in the living room on the phone with a 9-1-1 operator again.

He yelled, "Hey, I've just called!"

"They're on their way . . ." the dispatcher assured him.

Edwards was inconsolable. "I think someone killed my girlfriend. And her daughter's in her home, too. I just got home from work!"

"Okay, wait, hold on for a second," the Addison dispatcher responded, but Edwards raved on.

"I think they're dead! I'm not telling you a lie! I just walked in!"

"All right. Okay, okay, okay! Hold on! Just hold on!"

Edwards could hear the radio traffic in the background between the police dispatcher and patrol units.

"Three-oh-five."

"Three-oh-five, this will be assist the AFD, North Swift Road, Apartment [   ] . . . Complications with a pregnancy," droned the dispatcher.

Other units were checking in with their location and were instructed to proceed to the address.

The dispatcher told the units, "It seems like more of a problem at North Swift. Caller called back on nine-one-one saying that his girlfriend was all bloody and she seems lifeless."

Then he was back with Edwards, trying to calm him. "We've got them going, okay? You still there?"

"Yeah, man."

"Okay. Is she unconscious?"

"Yeah. I looked at her stomach! It's like I can see up in her stomach! Man, I ain't lying!"

"Okay, all right! I'm gonna stay on the line. . . ."

Edwards cut him short. "I've been calling her, everything, man! I don't know what's up! I just called my neighbors here! I just walked in!"

As the emotional spiel continued, the dispatcher advised patrol officers who were headed to the given address, "Subject is unconscious and appears lifeless. It was stated that one of the children is missing."

Then Edwards informed the dispatcher, "Hey, I think they're here. They're here, man! Do you want to talk to them?"

"No, no, you go talk to them."

Over the next few minutes, police officers and emergency paramedics poured into the modest apartment. They confirmed that the woman and the girl were dead. Besides the gruesome butchering, the woman had been shot in the back of the head.

No one was sure, but the paramedics and policemen suspected that the fetus was not inside the mother.

No one would know for certain until the autopsy was performed. No one, the cops realized, except the killer or killers of the pregnant mother. The police and the emergency personnel viewing the pitiful scene wondered what motive could possibly be behind the heinous slicing open of Debra Evans's abdomen. Ghoulish sadists, or, unimaginable as it seemed, had someone killed her to get the baby?

TWO

Across town, Detective Mark Van Stedum was sleeping soundly when the ringing phone jarred him awake shortly after 3:00 A.M. on Friday, November 17, 1995. The detective's supervisor, Sergeant Don Sommers, told him he was needed at the scene of a double homicide. Sommers gave the address on North Swift, and Van Stedum answered he would be there as fast as possible.

Detective hours sometimes are bad, but Van Stedum would not have any other job. Police work was in his blood. His father, Richard Van Stedum, only recently had retired after forty years as a Chicago police officer. Growing up on Chicago's northwest side, Van Stedum had heard plenty of "war" stories about police work during some of the action-filled years of his father's career—the Chicago riots, mob mayhem, his dad had seen it all.

The thirty-five-year-old detective also had other relatives who had been policemen.

"It's all I really knew," Van Stedum once mused. He was twenty-five years old when he took his first job as a police rookie with the Addison Police Department, after graduating from a Chicago high school and at-

tending Triton College in River Grove, a Chicago sub-
urb. He had degrees in police science and sociology.

After serving in the patrol division for three years,
he had been a detective going on seven years. Van
Stedum and his wife were used to the demands of his
job, which had no regimented hours when a major case
broke. His wife knew the demands; after all, they had
married while he was attending police academy.

Mrs. Van Stedum was glad the phone had not roused
their two sleeping kids. Like her, the children were long
accustomed, and immune, to the nighttime ring of the
telephone.

From the start of her husband's police career, Van
Stedum's wife did not ask questions about his job, and
he did not take his work home with him. He was careful to keep his family life and his police investigations
in two separate spheres.

It would be a long stretch before Van Stedum was
back home again.

Ambulances and police cars were parked around the
Pebble Ridge Apartments on North Swift when Van
Stedum arrived.

The brown three-story apartment building already
was roped off with yellow crime-scene tape, and uniformed men had been posted to secure the scene from
outsiders.

Sergeant Sommers was standing in front of the apartment when Van Stedum stepped from his car. The detective talked briefly with his supervisor, and Sommers
quickly filled in the basics: a double homicide, woman

and young girl. The woman had been nine months pregnant. Her abdomen bore a large eviscerating-type wound. It was uncertain whether the baby was still inside the slain mother.

Also, Sommers said a seven-year-old boy, brother of the slain girl, was missing.

Van Stedum and Sommers did a "walk-around" of the building, looking for possible evidence and the missing boy. Other officers took part in the search of the area.

Van Stedum glanced at a pair of shears that had been found on the sidewalk by one of the first officers on the scene. Appearing to be bloodstained, the shears were on the sidewalk just south of the front entrance that led to the apartment.

The patrolman had left the shears guarded until they could be photographed and placed in an evidence container. Detective Van Stedum observed that part of the handle was missing.

The large apartment complex consisted of several L-shaped buildings, surrounded by sidewalks, stretches of grass, and parking lots. There were trash Dumpsters in the parking areas that officers would need to search.

There also was a small swimming pool. The skyline view was interspersed with large power lines leading to various factories in nearby industrial parks, and a water tower bearing the words ADDISON, VILLAGE OF FRIENDSHIP.

When Van Stedum entered the apartment building, he saw a man holding a small boy and sitting on the inside stairway outside the door of the victim's apartment. The man gave his name as James Edwards. Standing nearby was the first officer to respond to the 911 call, Patrolman Don Browski.

The detective talked briefly with Edwards, who related how he came home from work and found the bodies.

Asked by the detective if he had any idea who might have done it, Edwards shook his head negatively. But he said his girlfriend, Debra, had been having trouble with a former boyfriend named Verne Ward and had obtained an order of protection against Ward.

Edwards said the legal protection document naming Ward might be in a dresser drawer in their bedroom.

When the detective saw Debra Evans's body, his first reaction was that she did not look nine months pregnant.

Van Stedum saw she was wet and bloody around her midsection. Her sweater was pulled down at this time and the stomach wound was not visible.

He could see stab wounds in her neck and blood spotted her face. Blood was pooled on the nearby love seat, and he noted the woman's blood had squirted on the end arm cushion.

The TV and a fan were on. A purse and scattered papers and other items were strewn over the love seat.

As he walked down a hallway to the bedrooms to look for the protection order described by Edwards, he saw more blood on the hall walls—again in spray patterns. Passing the bathroom, the detective saw squirts of blood all over the bathroom vanity, on the wall behind the vanity, and on the floor. The bathroom sink was blood-spattered, too.

In a small bedroom at the hall's end, he looked at the girl's body, her right arm flung outward. Her right palm was cut and bloody and there was another cut on her forearm, which he thought might be defensive wounds. She had been stabbed viciously.

There was more than one deep stab wound on the left side of her neck. A bloody towel was on top of her. A knit cap lay on her left shin.

Besides the bloodstained Pocahontas gown, she had on a pair of panties.

Other than the two sleeping pallets—one where Van Stedum assumed the missing boy slept—the small bedroom contained a miniature plastic pool table, a small desk with schoolbooks lying on top, a foam chair in front of a closet, a dresser, and some scattered stuffed animals.

In a larger bedroom, Van Stedum saw that the two adults apparently slept here in the queen-sized bed. Nearby was a miniature bed equipped with a net, probably where the smallest child slept.

Van Stedum went to the dresser to hunt for the legal paper that Edwards mentioned. He looked in the drawers but did not find it.

But he did come up with school pictures of the children. He particularly was glad to get the one of the missing boy to help with the search.

The detective noticed that the bedcover on the queen-sized bed was pulled down partly, as if one person might have been lying or sleeping there earlier. A telephone on the left side of the bed was pulled from the wall and the receiver was off the hook.

Near the phone he saw a bloody bubble-gum wrapper. He saw more blood on the right side of the bed and a blood-soaked Ace bandage lying on top of a man's sweatshirt on the bed.

He examined the windows and doors in the apartment to see if there was evidence of a forced entry, but he found no such signs.

After about fifteen minutes inside the apartment, Van Stedum went back to Edwards and asked him to accompany him to the police department for further questioning.

When they sat down in an office to talk, Edwards said he had been at work from about 5:30 P.M. Thursday until 2:40 A.M. Friday.

In a murder investigation, a spouse—or, in this case, a live-in boyfriend—routinely is suspect.

Yet, Van Stedum had a feeling after his brief conversation with the boyfriend that he was not involved in the murders. But he wanted to make sure and get on to other possibilities.

The detective went to another office and made a phone call to Edwards's employers at the factory where he worked. He confirmed that Edwards had been on the job steadily as he had said.

Later that morning, Detective Paul Hardt went to the factory and picked up copies of Edwards's time card and work sheet that cinched the fact he was on the job when he claimed. Not only that, interior security cameras showed him to be there.

Questioned briefly about his relationship with Evans,

Edwards told Van Stedum that they had lived together "off and on" since about 1986 or 1987. They had met, he said, when she was working temporarily at a nightclub in nearby Elgin, Illinois.

After they dated for several weeks, Edwards said, he began living with Debra and her two children in an apartment in Hanover. Joshua was about a year old and Samantha three.

They had separated several times during their relationship, but always mended their differences and went back together, the boyfriend said.

"How about Thursday—anything unusual come up before you left for work?" Van Stedum asked.

The day was mostly routine, Edwards recalled. They had gotten up about 9:00 A.M. They'd gone to the grocery store, buying groceries and some supplies that would be needed to care for the newborn infant when it was brought home.

Debbie, nine months pregnant, was planning to enter the hospital on Sunday evening to have the birth induced the next day. Edwards was arranging to take off from work and stay home to care for the other kids.

Edwards said Debbie had had an ultrasound about three weeks earlier that showed the infant was a boy. She had proudly posted the ultrasound photo on the front of the refrigerator in the kitchen. Van Stedum remembered seeing it.

They also had chosen a name for the infant: Elijah, or Eli for short.

Edwards recalled that Joshua and Samantha had come home from school the usual time in the afternoon, and a little neighbor boy whom Debbie regularly baby-sat had joined them.

Later, after the mother of the visiting boy had picked him up, the family had gathered at the small kitchen table for an evening meal of pizza.

Then Edwards had said good-bye, kissed Debbie on the cheek, and left about 5:30 P.M. for the short walk to his job, along North Swift Road that ran behind and on the west side of the apartment unit. The back door was on that side.

Just a routine day, Edwards said—until he came home and found the carnage.

The detective wanted to know more about Verne Ward.

Edwards said Ward was an ex-boyfriend of Evans's. In fact, he was the father of her youngest child, Jordan. Ward and Evans had lived together at various times. One time had been when Edwards and Evans were separated temporarily, Edwards said.

He told the detective that Ward had made harassing phone calls to Evans numerous times in the past, including several times during the last two weeks she was alive.

"Every time he called, there was an argument, basically," Edwards said. He said their heated phone conversations usually were about Jordan. In the past week, Evans finally had refused to talk to Ward when he phoned, Edwards recalled.

The interview with Edwards brought out information about the other children. Joshua, the missing boy, never knew his father. But Edwards said he and the boy had a good relationship. "He called me Daddy," said Edwards.

As for Samantha, Edwards had met her dad, Scott Gilbert, a nice guy who now lived in Florida. Her dad frequently visited or phoned Samantha, and the girl had visited him in Florida, said Edwards.

The detectives pressed the search for Verne Ward. Edwards had mentioned that Ward had been arrested previously in nearby Carol Stream.

Now, Van Stedum and his partner, Detective Mike Simo, hoped they might get Ward's mug shot, fingerprint card, and last known address from the Carol Stream police.

When they left to look for Verne Ward, the questioning of Edwards was turned over to Detectives Dave Wall and Cathy Vrchota, who sought additional information about the background of Evans and her relationships past and present.

Carol Stream was a short drive from Addison, and the homicide investigators arrived there about 7:00 A.M. Friday. The morning was cold and cloudy, and threatening rain or snow.

The police file on Laverne R. Ward disclosed a previous arrest on domestic battery charges that were remindful of his conduct with Evans, as it had been described by Edwards. On October 11, 1992, the Carol Stream police had busted Ward at a girlfriend's apartment after he violated an order of protection and beat her up. He also had attacked the police officers who came to the scene.

Placed on probation for two years, Ward later went to prison because he violated his probation by selling drugs. The Addison detectives learned that he had been released from the penitentiary last January after serving less than six months of a six-year sentence.

Ward was looming big as a suspect in the Evans family murders. The detectives got copies of Ward's mug shot and fingerprint card, and after trying to find him in Carol Stream, they returned to Addison.

There the search for the missing Joshua Evans had been expanded when daylight arrived.

Besides alerting all local and area patrol units to be on the lookout for the youth, the police department borrowed bloodhounds along with the dogs' special handlers.

Addison police officials also called in a helicopter equipped with an infrared scanner to assist in the hunt, which was first centered in the apartment complex area and then extended to surrounding neighborhoods.

THREE

At best, the investigators realized, it was a desperate race against time. They believed the boy had been abducted by the killer or killers. If this were so, they feared he had met the same fate as his mother and sister.

Having borrowed a family photo of Debbie, Samantha, Joshua, and Jordan from where it hung on a wall in the death apartment, the investigators had the picture copied and distributed to the Chicago-area newspapers and TV stations. The news media was glad to get the picture to go with the big story of the double homicide and apparent kidnapping in Addison.

Upon their return from Carol Stream, Detectives Van Stedum and Simo learned a new lead had been uncovered by the evidence technicians still going over the murder apartment on North Swift Road.

While checking Debra Evans's telephone Caller ID system, the evidence techs discovered that the last incoming call recorded on Thursday evening at 7:40 was listed to a woman at an address on Crescent Street in Wheaton, Illinois.

The detectives were thinking that the Wheaton caller might have been the last person whom Evans talked to before her brutal death.

The village of Wheaton is about thirty miles southeast of Addison. Both towns are in sprawling DuPage County, which has over 900,000 residents. Wheaton is the county seat.

Van Stedum and Simo drove to Wheaton and pulled up at the Crescent Street address about 10:30 A.M. The attractive young woman who answered the door identified herself as Tina Martin.

Van Stedum identified himself and his partner, and said they were investigating the death of a woman in Addison, Debra Evans. He asked about the phone call shown to have been made from this address that was on the victim's Caller ID register.

Martin answered that it was her cousin, Verne Ward, who had dialed Evans's number. She related that Ward, who lived nearby and did not have a phone, frequently dropped by her place to use the phone.

Martin lived with her mother and each of them had her own telephone.

She said Ward had used her mother's phone, located in the living room. Martin's separate phone line was in her bedroom.

Martin said that Ward had tried to reach Evans shortly after he had come by about 6:10 P.M. Thursday, but she apparently was not at home.

The living room phone had rung about an hour later.

Before Martin had been able to pick up the receiver, the answering machine had clicked on.

Martin said she had looked at the Caller ID and recognized it was that of her friend, Debbie Evans. She had dialed the number back.

Martin said, "I told her [Debbie] that it was Verne who called her, and then she asked me how my kids were doing, and I asked her how her kids were doing, and then I gave him the phone."

She had overheard part of the conversation, and she remembered one thing that Verne had said, "Is the baby mine, or is it his?"

She said Ward and Debbie had a lengthy conversation. After that, Ward had left Martin's home about 8:10 P.M., and Martin said she had not seen him since then.

She explained that she remembered the approximate time when Ward left because she was watching the TV program *New York Undercover,* which came on at 8:00 P.M. and had been on for ten minutes or so when he departed.

The detectives talked only briefly with Martin, who furnished Ward's current address and also the names and addresses of a couple of his girlfriends.

They first checked at Ward's apartment, but he was not there.

Next, going to one girlfriend's address given them by Martin, they were met at the door by a woman who said she had not seen him recently and didn't want to see him again.

"We broke up after a big argument," she said.

A short time later the detectives arrived at the other address. They found no one at home. As they were driving away, they spotted a car driven by a woman pull into the parking area.

The driver and a man who matched Ward's mug shot and description spotted them at the same time.

The man started scrambling into the backseat, apparently to get out of sight. The detectives quickly closed in. The passenger, who admitted he was Verne Ward, said he was trying to rearrange some things in the rear seat and was not trying to hide.

He agreed to accompany the detectives to the police station and talk to them.

The time was about noon on Friday, November 17, about the same time that a tip came to police in Villa Park, Illinois, another of the numerous western Chicago suburbs, that would break the hunt for Joshua Evans wide open.

Dwight Pruitt was a tough guy.

He was street tough and streetwise. His business was crime. He had pulled armed robberies. Right now he was on parole from an armed robbery rap. He also had fallen in the past on a charge of possession of a controlled substance, which in ordinary talk was being caught with dope.

He was a so-called "board member" of one of the toughest street gangs around, the Vice Lords, and had been a member for about eleven years.

For a large part of his life, the governing rule of the twenty-three-year-old Pruitt's existence had been to avoid policemen in any way possible. He didn't even want to watch cop shows. They made him nervous.

Now, Pruitt was about to do something he had never done in all of his action-packed criminal career. He was going to call the cops, which to his ilk was tantamount to John Dillinger dropping by the FBI office to say hello.

Around noontime on this Friday, November 17, Pruitt was watching a TV newscast in the Villa Park apartment where he lived with his girlfriend, Patrice, her two small daughters, and his and Patrice's six-week-old daughter.

Suddenly there was a picture on the screen of a little boy that grabbed Pruitt's attention. He recognized the boy. The kid had been in their apartment the night before and had had a miserable night. The picture that flashed on the screen was a family photo, with the boy, his mother, his sister, and little brother in it.

They looked like a nice family. They were smiling, except the smallest boy who was a serious-faced baby.

The guy giving the news was saying that the older boy, named Joshua Evans, was missing, the object of a big search.

The TV commentator said the police thought the boy had been taken by someone who had murdered the boy's mother and sister sometime last night in Addison, a town not far from Villa Park.

Pruitt and Patrice did not have a phone. Pruitt, who was not fully dressed, got up and put on his pants. He walked to the police trailer located in the apartment complex and found it closed. There was no cop there, for some reason.

So he walked to a nearby convenience store and asked the clerk if he could use the phone. The clerk said no, that there was a phone outside in the parking lot.

For the first time in his life that he was going to call the cops, Pruitt was having a hard time doing it.

He walked out to that telephone and discovered it wasn't working. How in the hell do you call a cop, anyway, Pruitt was thinking.

He gave up and went back to the apartment. Within a short time, Patrice returned. He told her, "That little boy that was here last night, they just showed a picture of him on TV and said the police are looking for him."

Something was very wrong with Patrice. She was white faced, didn't say anything, and looked like she was scared to death, Pruitt thought. He noticed also that the female friend whom Patrice had left with earlier was standing in the hall. They had taken the missing little boy, as well as Patrice's small daughter Lexis, with them.

Patrice took something out to the waiting woman. It looked like Ajax and a scrub brush. The woman took them and left, and he heard her car drive away.

Pruitt told his girlfriend he was going to try and find a phone again, if it could be done, and call the police. This time he went to the office of a nearby security alarm business, and was able to borrow their phone. He dialed the Villa Park Police Department.

When the police operator answered, Pruitt said, "I was looking at the news today, and I saw something about a murder, and they are looking for a little boy."

The operator said something that sounded like, "Hmmmm."

"I want the police to come by my home because I

think I know the little boy they are looking for," Pruitt said.

"You know the little boy they are looking for?" the operator asked.

"Yeah."

"Is he with you now, sir?"

"No, they just took him." Pruitt meant that Patrice and her female friend, who had brought the boy by their apartment late the previous night, had left earlier this morning to run some errands and had taken the little boy with them.

"Who just took him?" asked the police operator.

Pruitt's patience was growing short. "Will you just tell the police to come by my house." He was getting a little ticked off. He didn't know it was so hard to give some information to cops.

Not that he had ever wanted to before this. Usually, if he talked to any cop, he was doing his best to not put forth any information.

"Would you just tell the police to come by my house, because I think I know the little boy they are looking for. Will you just tell them to come by my house. I'll tell them the whole story."

"Okay, I'll tell them. You are in Villa Park?"

"Yeah, in Villa Park, Parliament Square." He gave the address and number of the apartment.

The operator repeated the address to Pruitt.

"Tell them I'll be waiting outside," Pruitt added.

"You'll be waiting in the parking lot?" the operator asked.

"I'll be waiting in front, right outside the building."

"Okay, stay on the line just a minute," said the operator. "And the phone number you are calling from?"

He gave the number and added, "I'm calling from a business pay phone."

"Your name please."

"Dwight Pruitt."

"Who has the little boy right now?"

Pruitt heaved a big sigh. "See, I wanted to be able to sit down and tell the police the whole story. Somebody brought him by our house and asked us to watch him. He was telling us that his mother got stabbed, and they came through the window, and I was watching the news today, and that little boy was just at my house."

"Just now?"

"Yes, they just took him, home or somewhere, about twenty minutes ago."

"Do you know where they went?"

"Yes. My girlfriend went with them, with the other woman who came over here to get him. My girlfriend is at home now, and if they would come over, she could tell them."

"So you are at your girlfriend's house, is that what you are saying?"

"No, I am saying I want the police to come to my house."

"I understand that, but I need to know where they went."

"I don't know, but my girlfriend could tell them, because she was with them."

"Is your girlfriend with them now, or is she at your house?"

"She is at my house."

"Okay, hold on one second. What apartment do you want them to go to? Are you going to meet them outside?"

"I am going to be standing outside."

"Okay. He is going to be standing outside. Hold on one second. What's your girlfriend's name, sir?"

"Patrice. Patrice Pruitt."

"What's her last name?"

"Scott, Pruitt."

"You know the date of her birth?"

"No."

"Did she get back twenty minutes ago, or they left twenty minutes?"

"She came back, she just got back."

"Okay."

"I was telling her that I had seen it on the news, and that was the little boy that she took out with her girlfriend . . . that dropped him over here [last night]. That's the little boy that was just over here, and he said that his parents were murdered. He was telling us just this morning when he woke up."

"Okay, do you know the little boy's name?"

"Joshua. It was just on the TV."

"Joshua?"

"Yes, Joshua."

"We're just sending the police now. Is everything okay? We are just telling them as you tell me, so just stay on the line for a second."

"Okay."

"What is your date of birth?"

"February 15, 1972."

"You just saw it on TV this morning, and you put it all together?"

"I like—you know, that can't be no coincidence. The same little boy and what he was describing to me, what had happened."

"Right."

"On TV," Pruitt said again for emphasis.

"And he was about eight years old, right?"

"Yes. He talked real good. He's about eight years old."

"He's a little black boy, white boy, Hispanic?"

"White."

"What's your apartment in the building, even though I know you are going to meet us outside?"

"Ground level." Pruitt gave the number again.

"They will be there in a minute. Just hold on."

"Just calling myself . . . being a Good Samaritan."

"That's very nice, actually, because that happened last night, right?"

"Yes, that's right, in Hanover Park."

"In Hanover Park?"

"I think it was. No, he didn't say it was, but when I heard the news this morning, it was just like it all matched, right?"

"Yes, this is what he was talking about. Do you know if your girlfriend knew the little boy?"

"No, her girlfriend just brung him over, asked us can we watch him, and this morning he was telling us what happened."

"This girlfriend just brought him over and asked you guys if you could watch him?"

"Yes, and he was telling us what happened this morning."

"Yeah."

"Then her girlfriend came back [this morning], and Patrice was asking her what happened, and she was giving a different story, and I was like—I don't believe her girlfriend—I believe this little boy. Because, you know, he don't have no reason to lie about it."

"Did he seem upset?"

"Yes, he was crying, saying, 'Mama's dead.' "

"Okay, you can stay on the line until the officers get there."

"Yes, I'll stay on the line."

"Great. Thanks."

Pruitt was not through talking. "You see, we have a police trailer, right here, and I went there to tell them, but nobody was there."

"Nobody was there? Does your girlfriend know you are calling?"

"I am going to tell her. I am going to tell that I am calling the police, because somebody is lying and it ain't the little boy. Because I've just seen it on the news talking about it. And it ain't no coincidence. He said his mother had a black boyfriend, and a little baby that wasn't hurt, and she was pregnant."

"Hold on a second."

"The police are here, out front."

"Go ahead, if you want to go ahead and talk to them."

"Okay, and thank you."

FOUR

The police unit pulled up at the alarm company office from where Pruitt had phoned. He got into the car, and they drove the short distance to the apartment on Parliament Square. Already, a patrolman and two detectives were there trying to talk to Scott, who was sobbing hysterically.

Pruitt tried to calm his out-of-control girlfriend and get her to answer the police questions. The officers kept asking the woman where they took the little boy. All she could do was cry, her head in her hands.

"Tell them, Patrice, tell them!" Pruitt said harshly. "You've got to tell them! They want to know where they took the little boy!"

"Can you take us to where they left the little boy?" one detective suggested.

Still crying loudly, she nodded and said she would try.

Patrice Scott eventually would make a lengthy statement about the terrifying events that began in her Villa Park apartment early that Friday morning.

The story related by Scott—combined with what the investigators already knew had happened in the Evans apartment in Addison—would be described later by an assistant state's attorney as "like something out of a Stephen King novel."

With the clock moving toward 1:00 A.M. on Friday, November 17, Scott and her boyfriend Pruitt were in bed watching the TV show, *In the Heat of the Night*. In another bedroom of the apartment they shared in Villa Park were Scott's two small daughters, six and seven years old. A tiny baby girl, Alexis, born to the couple only a few weeks earlier, was asleep nearby.

Suddenly they heard knocking at a front window in the living room. Pruitt got out of bed, put on his robe, and went to the window. When he looked out, he could not see who was there.

He went up a short flight of stairs to the front door. He could now see that it was a female friend of Patrice's standing outside. There was a little boy with her.

He did not admit them, but came back to the bedroom and told Patrice, "Your friend Annette is at the door." Then he returned to bed and resumed watching the TV program.

Scott slipped into a robe and went upstairs to the front entrance. Standing outside was Annette Williams and a small blond-headed boy whom Patrice did not know. When she opened the door, Scott noticed a four-door gray car parked at an angle in front of the building. Williams's boyfriend, Fedell Caffey, was in the front seat on the driver's side. She also saw a baby's car seat in the car.

Annette Williams was dressed in a Starter coat with

a sweater underneath. Scott noticed what looked like blood on the sweater.

Williams asked if the boy could spend the night, hastily explaining that his mother "had been shot in a drug deal that went bad," and adding that she was going to the hospital to see about her. "I'll pick him up in the morning," Williams said.

"Okay, he can spend the night," Scott replied. She didn't ask any questions, thinking the blood on the sweater might have something to do with the hospitalized injured mother of the boy.

Her friend's words about "a drug deal gone bad" did not particularly surprise Scott, either.

She did not know who the boy's mother was, or whether she did or didn't have anything to do with "a drug deal gone bad." But she knew that Caffey, Williams's live-in boyfriend, was involved in drugs—pushing crack cocaine—and that Annette herself was an occasional crack user.

"Go with my friend," Williams told the boy. She started to run back to the waiting car, but then turned and said, "I had my baby last night. I'll bring him over in the morning when I come back to get the boy."

Scott couldn't help but wonder how Annette could be so active after giving birth just "last night" and now going to be with this little boy's mother. She should be recuperating herself, Scott thought. She was surprised by Williams's announcement, which seemed to come almost as an afterthought, even though her friend had been saying she was expecting just anytime.

Scott and Williams had things in common, though

Patrice was not a drug user. The strongest habit she could own up to was drinking "coolers."

They both were in their late twenties, had three children, and lived with boyfriends who were lawbreakers. Yet, both women led ordinary domestic lives, regularly engaged in housecleaning; getting their kids off to school; attending school activities; doing occasional baby-sitting, grocery shopping, and all that goes with being a dutiful housewife and mother.

In the past the two women had shared an apartment for a short time. When Scott got a new boyfriend, Pruitt, the women didn't get together as often, although they visited back and forth and talked on the phone. Their lives were a paradoxical combination of being normal housewives and mothers and yet living with men who had moved in the Chicago area's dark hinterlands of drug dealing and street gang activity.

Yet, their boyfriends usually were kind toward their children, those they had fathered and those born of other men who had passed that way.

In a sense the two women—and other women who found themselves in similar relationships—lived in a twilight zone of the good and the bad.

As Scott and the boy walked downstairs to the ground-level part of the apartment, she asked the boy his name.

"Joshua," he replied.

"My name is Patrice," Scott said, smiling.

Joshua mentioned he had to go to the bathroom, and Scott showed him where it was. While he was gone, she got a sheet, blanket, and pillow and made him a sleeping place on the black couch next to a wall. When Joshua returned, Scott pointed to the couch where he would sleep. He said nothing, but took off his brown boots and his green coat. Still wearing a long red T-shirt, he crawled under the cover.

After making sure the door was locked again, Scott went back to bed. Briefly she told Pruitt what Williams had said.

Later—she wasn't sure of the time—Scott was awakened by her baby crying. She was getting up to tend to the infant when she heard the little boy whimpering and moaning. She found that he was asleep but apparently having a nightmare.

About 5:00 A.M., when it was time for her feeding, Alexis really started crying. Scooping the infant from her bed and murmuring soothing words, the mother took her into the living room and laid her on the couch while she prepared her bottle.

Joshua still was going on in his sleep, crying and moaning. Scott remained up because her baby would not go to sleep. She sat on the couch and held and rocked the infant in her arms, humming a low tune.

Joshua came fully awake about the time Scott's other daughters were getting up and dressing for school. He sat up suddenly and started crying and talking at the same time.

"What's the matter, honey, are you worried about your mom?" Scott asked, putting her arm around him. "She's going to be all right."

"No, no, she's not!" the youngster sobbed. "She's dead and so is my sister. Some burglars came through the window, and they cut my mom and my sister. You've got to go get my little brother. He's still there! My stepfather don't know where he is!"

When she asked where he lived, he said the Pebble Ridge Apartments in Addison.

"I know where that is," Scott said.

The boy said over and over as tears rolled down his face that his mommy and sister were dead—cut and killed by the burglars.

"How many burglars?" Scott asked.

"Four," he answered.

"Do you know who they were?"

His answer was shocking.

"It was Annette, Fedell, and Verne!" the boy cried, breaking into uncontrollable weeping again.

She asked if he knew the fourth burglar. His reply was hard to understand because of his crying, but it sounded like "Bo Bo" or "Boo Boo," an indistinguishable nickname or something.

But he kept repeating the other three names—Annette, Fedell, and Verne. "They grabbed my mommy and cut her and my sister. They're dead, they're dead, and my little brother is there! You've got to get him!"

The boy said he had hidden, and when the burglars left, he had run out the back door and Annette had grabbed him, and they had taken him to this house.

Dwight Pruitt came out of the bedroom. On his way to the kitchen to get some juice, he paused and spoke to the crying boy.

"Hi, my name's Dwight. What's your name?"

"Joshua," came the muffled answer. Pruitt had heard the sorrowful words of the boy, repeated over and over:

"Burglars . . . came through a window . . . cut my mommy and my sister . . . bloody, dead."

Pruitt was frowning as he sat down at the dining room table. "Patrice, what this little boy is telling us is different from what your friend said last night. What's going on?"

Before she could say anything, her daughters came into the room. Seeing the emotional state of the boy, one girl asked if he would like for her to read to him. Still crying, he nodded. The girls went to their bedroom and came back with the book *The Lion King*.

Joshua calmed some as the book was read. The girls talked with him about the pictures in the book, trying to keep him from thinking of those terrible things he had been saying.

When it was time for the girls to go to school, Scott told them to get their coats and books and go to the other side of the building to see if the lady who gave them a ride to school was ready.

As they left, Joshua said, "Put the chain back on the door. The burglars might come back!" He sobbed.

Scott replaced the chain.

Around ten o'clock someone knocked at the front window. Scott looked out and saw Annette Williams. She went upstairs to let her in. Williams was dressed differently this morning and had on a long green spandex dress.

Scott closed the door after her friend entered, secured it, and confronted Williams immediately with what Joshua had said about his mother and sister.

"Annette, what you told me happened to his mom—she was in the hospital—that's not what Joshua is saying. He's saying something different. He says burglars killed his mom and sister. He says it was you, Fedell, and Verne."

Williams scowled angrily and shouted at Joshua, "What are you over here telling this shit? You talk too fucking much! Shut your fucking mouth!"

"No, no, no! That's what happened!" the boy cried. "That's what happened! That's what happened! You were there! You and them killed my mommy and Sam! I saw you! I saw you!"

Williams's temper exploded again. "You talk too damn much! You got a big mouth!"

Then Williams asked Scott to get a glass of water so Joshua could take some medicine that his mother had left for him in Williams's car.

"What medicine? I don't take any medicine!" the boy blurted.

Williams took the boy and the glass of water into the kitchen. The boy must have swallowed whatever it was because Scott heard him gagging and choking.

"Go to the bathroom and spit it up!" Williams yelled at him.

The boy dashed to the bathroom, and Scott heard him gagging and puking in the bathroom. In a few minutes the white-faced and sick-looking Joshua came back and sat down on the couch where he had slept. His face was distorted in anguish and something else, terror. Scott thought she smelled iodine.

The suffering boy pulled his T-shirt down over his

legs and stared silently at the women who were seated across from him on another couch.

Scott asked Williams, "What's going on? Why is he saying these things he's saying?" Was it the ravings of a terror-stricken youngster who had actually witnessed a horrible crime? Or the recounting of terrible nightmares of an imaginative child worried about his injured mother?

"He talks too damn much!" Williams said heatedly. She ordered Joshua: "Turn around and face the front!"

When he was facing the other way, Williams said, "Fedell told me to take him out south by the Projects and leave him."

Scott knew about the so-called South Projects, an overcrowded, crime-ridden urban housing project for the poor where drug dealing was rampant.

"Why do something like that?" Scott responded. "Something terrible would happen to him out there Why don't you just take him to the police station so they can take him by some relative's house or something?"

Williams ignored the question and changed the subject, now talking about Scott's recently born daughter, telling the new mother that she had a baby bag and a hat and some baby outfits for the tiny girl.

Williams especially wanted Scott to go with her to see her own new baby boy, whom she had said was born last night.

"Okay," Scott said, getting up. "Okay, I'm going to ask Dwight if he will watch Lexis for me until I get back."

When she went to the bedroom with her request,

Pruitt said he was still sleepy and trying to sleep, and he told her not to go. He was concerned about the whole situation that had been dropped in their lap.

His attitude made Scott mad. She flared, "Why? You never want me to go anywhere." She stomped from the room and dressed the baby and herself to accompany Williams.

She would regret her decision for a long time.

FIVE

Scott, with Lexis in her arms, Williams, and the silent and frightened Joshua left the Villa Park apartment in a car driven by Williams. It looked like the same four-door gray car Scott had seen angle-parked in front of the building when Williams first dropped by to leave the boy.

Williams drove, with Scott and baby Lexis in front with her. Joshua, wearing undershorts and a red T-shirt, which he had slept in, and his green coat and brown boots but without jeans, was in the backseat. He was quiet now, apparently fearful to say anything.

Leaving Scott's place, Williams drove around the corner and stopped at a liquor store. The women—Scott carrying her baby—went inside. Joshua stayed in the car. Scott bought some cigarettes and juice, and Williams purchased a grape soda.

Returning to the car, Williams poured part of the grape pop into a cup and gave it to Joshua. He gulped it down hurriedly. His insides were burning terribly from the "medicine" Williams had made him drink in Scott's kitchen, but he was afraid to say anything about it.

Arriving at her home, Williams raised the garage

door with an automatic opener, drove inside, and then put the door down.

"Get out and come in for a while," Williams said. "I'll get my baby ready, and you can see him."

Williams led the way up some stairs and into the living room. Scott laid Lexis on a couch, and Joshua sat down and started playing with some cartridges for a game he found on the floor.

Williams yelled down from upstairs, telling Scott to look around the house since that was the first time she had been there.

Needing to feed Lexis, Scott looked in the kitchen for a can opener to open a can of milk but couldn't find one.

She was still searching when Williams called out, "Patrice, come on upstairs."

"In here," Williams directed. Scott entered a bedroom where she saw Fedell Caffey, a slender man with a thin mustache, lying in bed. He was holding a tiny baby with strands of blond hair showing from underneath a small baby cap.

Williams stood next to the bed.

When Williams picked up the sleeping infant and handed him to her, the baby's T-shirt pulled up and Scott noticed there was a piece of tape across the navel area.

"Fedell accidentally knocked loose the umbilical cord," Williams explained, adding, "Isn't he precious? You think he looks like his daddy?" She was referring to Caffey.

Scott politely answered yes, thinking the infant really

was too little to look like anything except a puckered-up newborn baby.

Holding the baby in her arms, Williams opened a closet door, indicating a can of baby formula on a shelf and baby clothes, a baby car seat carrier and other baby items. She asked Scott to hold the baby, then removed the baby carrier from the closet and took back the sleeping infant, laid him on the bed and started dressing him.

While her friend was thus occupied, Scott went downstairs to check on her own baby, as well as Joshua. Then she renewed her hunt in the kitchen for a can opener.

Williams came in with her baby in the car seat carrier. She set it down and located an opener, opened a can of milk and put it in the microwave to fill bottles for both babies.

It was a domestic scene, two mothers chatting as they prepared to feed their babies. Joshua remained silent and seated in the living room.

There was nothing about the homey scene to forewarn of the heinous acts about to happen.

Using her baby's blanket, Scott propped up the bottle so her infant could drink. Meanwhile, Williams went downstairs to a basement room. Shortly, Scott heard her call up the stairs, asking her to bring Joshua and come down.

At the bottom of the stairway, Scott and the boy went into a laundry room that was equipped with a washer and dryer; clothing was scattered over the floor. There was also a black metal-frame daybed against one wall.

As they entered, Williams told Joshua to sit on the daybed. Fedell Caffey also was there, and he was talking to another man, whom Scott did not recognize.

After conversation between Caffey and the other man, to which Scott paid no attention, the visitor said he had to leave to take care of some business. Caffey escorted him out through the garage.

When Caffey came back, Williams began telling her boyfriend what Joshua had said to Scott and Pruitt.

"He's got a big mouth," the scowling Williams said. "He talks too much. He knows our names. He said my name, your name, and Verne's name."

"Why didn't you take him out south where I told you to take him?" Caffey asked. He was angry. He gestured toward Scott and asked, "Why did you bring that bitch over here?"

Williams did not reply. She picked up what looked like a white cord. She walked over to where Joshua was sitting on the daybed and ordered him to "lean forward and stick your neck out."

The boy looked terrified, but he did as he was told.

Then, Williams suddenly looped the cord around Joshua's neck, and as Scott watched in horror, Williams and Caffey each grabbed an end of the rope and started pulling.

Joshua was screaming and tearing at the cord, trying to get it off his neck. His face was turning red. Right before her eyes, they were strangling the helpless child to death!

Scott screamed and acted impulsively, pushing Williams away as hard as she could. She saw the enraged look on Caffey's face, but he dropped his end of the cord.

The livid-faced Williams stormed up the stairs. But a minute later she returned, and Scott saw that the still angry woman was holding a long, rusty knife with a brown handle behind her back!

Scott screamed. "No . . . no . . . no . . . please! Please let him go and take me home! I want to go home! Please, can I take Joshua with me? I won't say nothing."

Williams threw the knife on the daybed.

Scott, her voice quivering, asked: "Can I go upstairs and get my baby?"

Williams turned to Caffey. "She won't tell. Let her go. Let me take her home."

Caffey said slowly and with cold menace, "If you open your damn mouth and tell anybody, I'll kill you! I'll kill your whole family! I'm not playing games!"

Joshua lay sideways on the daybed, crying hysterically and rubbing his neck. There were livid marks from the rope on it. Scott was crying and filled with fear for herself and the boy.

All that the little boy had said while in her apartment the night before and early this morning rang in her ears.

She had not known then whether Josh was reciting a nightmare or telling how he had actually witnessed the gruesome murders of his mother and sister by her friend and her boyfriend and two other men.

If only she had believed the boy, they would not be here now. But at the time she could not bring herself to even think that Annette Williams would do something like that.

"Take her home!" Caffey said. He stared at Scott and said, "Get the hell out of here and keep your mouth shut!"

Scott took Joshua by the hand and they stumbled up the stairs. He was still crying and rubbing his neck.

The shaking Scott looked at a door they passed and saw what she thought was a padlock on it. She knew she couldn't open it.

Williams had followed them up the stairway, saying nothing. She picked up her baby and his bottle, and said, "I'm going to take you home. We need to go back downstairs and out the way we came through the garage."

Scott was filled with renewed fear as she went downstairs again, Lexis gripped tightly in her arms. The women exchanged no words as they descended to the lower level and entered the garage again.

Caffey, silent now, joined them as they walked to the gray car. Scott holding Lexis got in the right front seat.

Caffey was in the backseat, and Williams ordered Joshua to get back there.

Scott looked back and saw Williams also had partially entered the backseat. She was in the back, but not sitting down. It appeared that she was holding Joshua on the floorboard with his arm pinned down.

She saw Caffey suddenly raise the big knife and plunge it downward. In stark terror, fighting against fainting, Scott turned back to the front to her baby, Lexis, who was screaming and crying. At the same time she felt the boy kicking desperately against the back of her seat, making gagging noises. Then the kicks against the seat stopped.

Annette Williams got into the front driver's side and closed the door. She ignored the weeping Scott.

Scott heard Caffey tell Williams, "You know where to go."

Lexis continued to cry and scream, as if she were aware of what had happened. Caffey told Scott to keep her baby quiet. He said it several times. She heard Joshua whimper, not loud at all, a diminishing whimper and moan. Scott was afraid she was going to throw up.

The garage door went up and the car pulled out of the garage. Scott knew they were traveling along a highway, but she did not have any idea where they were going until she spotted a sign that said MAYWOOD, the name of a town not far from Schaumburg, where the trip of horror had begun.

Williams drove to a semi-isolated location and finally stopped. She got out, and she and Caffey pulled Joshua from the back. One on each side of the little boy, they walked him down a gangway leading to an alley behind a building.

It wasn't like the boy was walking, more as if they were holding him up and force-walking him into the shadowy corridor.

Scott stayed in the car, too terrified to move or try to flee. She held her baby against her and wept.

In a few minutes, Williams and Scott returned. Joshua was not with them.

Williams got behind the wheel to drive and Caffey got in back. At this point, Scott, numb with icy terror, was not sure whether she and her baby would live or not.

She heard Caffey tell Williams to drop him off. Before Caffey got out somewhere in Maywood and walked away, Williams told him threateningly, "You better not go to that bitch's house!"

Caffey didn't respond to the remark, but he turned and told Scott, "You better keep your damn mouth shut!"

Williams gunned the car's motor and drove off angrily.

"You wouldn't understand," Williams said to Scott. She concentrated on the driving and remained quiet.

Right then Scott wasn't trying to understand. She only wanted to get Lexis and herself away from the violent madness she had witnessed, away from the unbelievable cruelty and murderous savagery that that poor little boy had endured before they dragged him from the car and left him in a dark alley.

It would be a cold and wet alley, for now sleet was falling.

She was sure that if he were still alive when they supported him on each side and disappeared into the murky gangway, he was not alive when they left him there finally.

Scott could hardly believe it when Williams pulled up at the Villa Park apartment.

Scott had been trying to act normal, as if nothing had happened, until she could get out of this hellish car and away from this fiendish woman whom Scott thought she had known as a typical housewife, mother, and friend. Annette already had three children before this new baby.

She wanted to get to Dwight and tell him about the unimaginable events she had witnessed.

When Williams stopped at the Parliament Street apartment, they all got out of the car and walked to some bushes near the front window of Scott's apartment. It was where any visitor first knocked so they could be let into the front entrance one level above the window—the window that Annette had knocked on about 1:00 A.M. this day.

Williams tapped on the window.

It was a worried-looking Dwight Pruitt who opened the front door. Scott with her baby went inside with Pruitt, and Williams stayed outside. Moving away where Williams would not hear him, Pruitt immediately started telling his girlfriend, "Patrice, you know that stuff the little boy was telling us last night? God, it must be true. It was on the news with a picture of him and his mamma and sister and another little boy. This TV guy said Joshua was missing and his mamma and sister were murdered, and there's a big hunt going on now for the little boy, Joshua."

Scott, emboldened by the protective presence of Pruitt, stepped outside and told Williams, "Joshua's family picture and what happened to them was on the news, Dwight said."

"When?" Williams asked.

"A little while ago," Scott replied.

"Do you have some cleaning stuff and rags or something I can borrow? I got to clean up some baby vomit in the car."

Scott, wanting to get rid of Williams as fast as possible, ran to a closet and got a can of Ajax and a scrub brush and gave them to the waiting woman.

In a few seconds she heard Williams drive off.

Scott burst into loud sobbing. Pruitt told her he had tried to call the police after hearing the noon news, but had been unable to find a phone he could use.

"I'm going to call them back now," he said. "Get back inside and lock the door and don't open it for anybody except me and the police."

Scott went into their apartment and collapsed on the couch, weeping hysterically.

Before long some Villa Park policemen arrived and Pruitt also returned, accompanied by a police officer.

They asked her questions, but mainly they wanted to know where Joshua Evans had been left.

After composing herself as much as she could, Scott and her boyfriend left with two detectives in a police car for her to try to find the spot where Joshua had been pulled from the gray car and walked or carried into an entrance to an alley.

SIX

The autopsy on Debra Evans confirmed that the full-term fetus had been removed by her killer or killers. Whether the infant was born alive or dead was open to conjecture, but medical experience leaned heavily toward it being stillborn.

Dr. Shakku Teas, a pathologist who had done hundreds of autopsies, received a call Friday morning from the DuPage County Coroner's Office to do the autopsies on Evans and her daughter, Samantha. She drove to the Medical Examiner's building in the group of DuPage County government buildings on North County Farm Road in Wheaton, the county seat.

Victims of violence come into the county morgue still wearing the clothing they had on at the time of their death—if they were dressed—and still covered with blood from their wounds. Bodies are refrigerated until autopsies can be performed.

Dr. Teas carefully removed the brown paper bags from Evans's hands—placed there by investigators to preserve any forensic evidence that might be under the fingernails or on the skin—and another bag on her head that covered a gunshot wound.

Earlier X rays had revealed the bullet was still inside

Evans's head. She was dressed in a gray sweater with stripes, gold-colored pants, and black bra and panties.

After photographing the body as brought to the table, Teas removed the bloodstained clothing.

The body of the twenty-eight-year-old woman was weighed and measured: Evans weighed 220 pounds and was five feet five inches in height. There was blood on her hair, her neck, and the lower part of the body.

After removal of the clothing and completion of blood tests for sexual assault, the body was thoroughly washed with soap and water before examination of the bullet and cut and stab wounds began.

Since the X ray disclosed the bullet at the front of the skull, the pathologist looked for the entry hole in the back of the head. She found it slightly right of midline and was able to trace its path and recover the slug from behind the right forehead region.

Teas learned that the bullet had gone through the right side of the woman's brain—actually had damaged all of that side. When she removed the bullet, Teas turned and handed it to evidence technician Jim Guenther of the DuPage County Sheriff's Office, who put it in an evidence bag. Guenther was present in the autopsy room to collect what evidence might be found and to take it to the crime laboratory.

The doctor also located four cut wounds in Evans's neck—called incise wounds because they are not as deep as stab wounds. In the parlance of pathology, the types of cut wounds are differentiated.

Stab wounds are described as deeper and longer than an incise wound. A wound about an inch long and two inches deep is a stab wound. Comparatively, an incise wound usually is longer than it is deep. Both types had been inflicted on Debra Evans's body—the incise wounds being superficial cuts.

There was a large gaping wound in Evans's lower abdomen. The horizontal wound was just above the pubic region. It measured thirteen inches in length and extended from one side to the other of her stomach. Fat could be seen coming out of the opening.

Part of the umbilical cord was sticking out. The cord had been cleanly cut, indicating a sharp instrument had been used. Two other shallow wounds were visible right above and parallel to the gaping horizontal cut. One measured about seven inches; the other less than two inches.

Edges of the large stomach wound showed superficial areas of incision—which to the pathologist meant that somebody had a change of mind and moved to another area to make the cut.

When the pathologist opened up the body and examined the uterus, she saw an opening about five inches long in the lower part. The fetus was gone. A pregnant uterus stretches to a great degree, which would have allowed the fetus to be withdrawn through the opening.

The doctor saw that a placenta still was attached to the uterus itself. The placenta is a vascular organ connected to the embryo by the umbilical cord, and it is the structure through which the embryo receives nourishment.

Also, one intestine near the uterus had been partly cut.

Photographs taken during each step of the autopsy would be available later to investigators and trial jurors.

Finishing the autopsy, the pathologist concluded that the main cause of death was the gunshot wound to the head, with the multiple stab and incise wounds contributing to Evans's death.

If bleeding had continued unchecked, the major abdomen wound alone would have been fatal.

Judging from the irregular edges of the body cuts, a pair of poultry shears found by police outside the apartment could have been the murder instrument, Teas believed.

Based on the cuts' irregular edges, Teas reported they were inflicted "by an instrument that is more blunt than a knife—a sharp instrument but a little blunt, not a nice knife that is really sharp—which would be consistent with something like scissors or shears."

Later, after the autopsy, Addison detectives discussed with Dr. Teas the chance of a full-term fetus surviving after being removed from a pregnant mother who might already have been dead.

"How long could the baby survive—if it was a full-term baby born after the mother's heart quit beating—and without suffering brain damage from oxygen deprivation?" one investigator asked.

"Yes, I think that is possible because the heart pumps for a few minutes after the mother's death," Teas said. "It depends on what you call death, because what it means to me is that death is a process. It is not as if a person who is shot drops dead at once. It might be that the heart is still beating and pumping blood, even though the person is unconscious. If the heart is still beating, the fetus would be okay."

Asked what the time frame would be, the doctor said, "Usually the brain could sustain anoxia (deprivation of oxygen) for three minutes, five minutes, which is a long time."

The detectives wondered which had happened first—the gunshot to the head or the cut wounds in the abdomen. Teas said there was no way she could tell by looking at the wounds.

"But correlating the wounds with the scene might help," she suggested.

She referred to the blood spatter on the body. "If the cut wounds on the abdomen had been made before the gunshot, they would have been extremely painful if the victim were still alive, and she would have struggled or tried to push away the assailant."

This physical movement would result in blood spatter patterns at the scene that might help determine if the woman was alive when she was cut so horribly, the doctor thought.

The pattern in which the blood spatter fell would depend on the body movement, she said.

When the autopsy findings were correlated later with the forensic evidence at the apartment crime scene, and with experts' opinions about the type of blood spatter patterns, the investigators would have a clearer picture as to whether Debra Evans was alive or not when the brutal makeshift cesarean section was performed on the living room floor.

* * *

Dr. Teas's autopsy findings for ten-year-old Samantha Evans suggested that she died fighting for her life. So-called defensive wounds were discovered on the girl's sixty-six pound, four-feet-five-inch body.

When the body was wheeled to the autopsy table, the girl still was clad in a pair of "printed" panties and a bloody nightgown with the cartoon figure of Pocahontas on it. Both of her hands and her long hair were covered with brown sacks attached by evidence technicians who worked the crime scene.

There was blood on the girl's face, neck, and hands. After the small body was undressed and washed thoroughly, the pathologist began probing and measuring the incisive cuts and deeper stab wounds in the neck and throat.

Teas found seven wounds in the girl's neck and throat—located in the right, center, and left areas of the neck. The worst was a gaping hole in the side of her neck.

The weapon's thrust had cut through the large muscle that protects the vital organs of the neck. The stabbing instrument had severed the main artery, the nerve, and the vein that brings blood back from the face and head area to the heart. Also badly cut was the nerve that comes from the brain and goes downward to actually control the heart, the lungs, and many of the abdominal organs. The jugular vein was cut, and the deep stroke of the weapon had gone through the vertebral column and fractured the fifth vertebra. The vicious thrust also had cut through the vertebral artery, which takes blood to the brain.

Both of Samantha's hands bore defensive wounds. A

cut about one-half inch long and one-half inch deep on her left forearm and a superficial cut on her right upper leg were classified as "defensive wounds," or those sustained when a victim is trying to resist and fight off an attacker. The cuts on her hands probably happened when the girl grabbed at the weapon or tried to push it away. From the wounds' rough edges, Teas believed shears or scissors inflicted the cuts. The pathologist ruled the cause of Samantha Evans's death was "multiple knife wounds."

The tests on both victims to determine if they had been sexually assaulted were negative.

The savage attacks on the pregnant mother and her ten-year-old daughter appalled the homicide detectives. They surmised there could have been only one reason to kill the girl: remove a witness. The killing had been cold-blooded and extremely brutal.

Had Joshua Evans not been hiding, he, too, probably would have been slain in the apartment. Only tiny Jordan Evans had been spared, probably because his age removed any chance of his being an effective witness.

There was another reason, too, why Jordan was not killed, but that would not come to light until the identity of the killers was known.

Although he was left alive, Jordan, who wandered through the blood of his mother and sister in the silent apartment until James Edwards came home and found him bloody and crying, had suffered emotional trauma that would affect him for months afterward.

The Chicago area, with its history of violent murder going back to the rampant mobster days of the '20s and '30s, had seen nothing like the Evans family murders since the so-called "crime of the century," when a drifter named Richard Speck raped and slaughtered eight student nurses on July 14, 1966.

Like the Speck massacre, the Addison murders would make big headlines and shocking television news segments, not only in the Chicago area and the rest of the United States but around the world.

The heinous slayings and the unimaginable kidnapping of an infant from the mother's womb even brought forth a statement by Speaker of the House Newt Gingrich in the nation's capital. Six days after the homicides, Gingrich blamed the Addison murders on "the welfare state" and the moral failure of America's leaders.

Ironically, the Evans murders were not the first to have happened in the apartment in Addison. The brutal rape-murder of another woman had taken place there. Veteran policemen and longtime residents recalled the sex killing of Lillian LaCrosse on April 17, 1985.

There were haunting parallels in the two cases. LaCrosse was a young housewife and the mother of three small children. Her husband went to work at 10:00 P.M., and when he returned the next day at 7:30 A.M., he found his wife's seminude body on the floor of the dining room of their apartment in North Swift. She was wearing only her shirt, had been sexually assaulted, and stabbed at least twenty-five times. There was evidence the woman also had been strangled.

The victim's purse and a movie camera were missing from the apartment.

One of the LaCrosse case investigators had been Officer Barry Muniz of the Addison Police Department, who now was working as an evidence technician in the Evans murder.

During the LaCrosse investigation, Muniz found blood in the victim's kitchen, on a dresser in the bedroom where the purse was taken, in a hallway leading from the LaCrosse apartment, and on the landing inside the entrance to an apartment building next door.

When the Addison police executed a search warrant for an apartment in the adjacent building, they found blood on the refrigerator and the bathtub.

Darryl Simms, a neighbor who lived in that apartment, was arrested and later convicted of murder, aggravated sexual assault, armed robbery, home invasion, and residential burglary.

He was sentenced to death, and is still on Illinois death row.

SEVEN

When Detectives Van Stedum and Simo returned to the Addison Police Department with Laverne Ward, they did not learn much from questioning him.

He denied knowing anything about the Evans killings. He said he spent Thursday drinking, had locked himself out of his apartment, and then visited various relatives and friends.

He admitted to making the phone call to Evans from Tina Martin's apartment, but said it was a friendly call and that Evans even had made him laugh during their talk.

Checking out Ward's alibi was interrupted by another development.

Police investigators in Maywood notified the Addison detectives of a search being made for the missing Joshua Evans in an area where the towns of Maywood and Bellwood adjoin. It started after a man in nearby Villa Park phoned the police there and said he knew something about the little boy whose picture he had just seen on a TV newscast.

Detective Van Stedum left immediately for the search

scene. When he arrived shortly after 2:00 P.M., Addison detectives Dave Wall and Joe Lullo already were there, along with officers from Maywood, Bellwood, and Villa Park.

With them was Dwight Pruitt, the man who had given the tip, and his girlfriend, Patrice Scott, who was holding her baby.

Van Stedum learned that Pruitt had called the Villa Park police and said he recognized the missing Joshua from a TV newscast photo. The boy had been left at his and Scott's apartment about 1:00 A.M. that day by Annette Williams, a friend of Scott's.

The nightmarish events that followed later that morning in Williams's residence in Schaumburg were related later by Scott to the Villa Park officers who responded to Pruitt's phone call. The hysterical Scott had agreed to try and take the police to where Joshua had been dumped in an alley after being stabbed.

Scott was unable to pinpoint the exact spot where she said Joshua had been removed from a car and taken into an alley, but she recalled the general area where the search now was being made.

As he helped with the search, Van Stedum received a terse radio message from Detective Wall. The boy's body had been found. It was in an alley behind 21st Street in Maywood.

Driving to the address, Van Stedum parked nearby and entered the alley. Among the officers present was Lieutenant Harold Jenkins, the day watch commander who had been dispatched from the Maywood Police Department.

The pitiful sight of the youngster hit Van Stedum hard. He had kids of his own. He saw the boy's body sprawled facedown like a broken and discarded life-sized doll.

He lay close to the back of a house, clad in a red T-shirt, red and green undershorts, short brown hiking boots, and a lengthy green coat.

The coat was pulled up partly over his upper body and head, not quite covering his blond hair. There was blood on his underwear. He lay amid patches of leftover snow and dead leaves. Van Stedum did not examine the body closely because the scene had not been processed for possible evidence.

Evidence technician Dean Beville of the Cook County Sheriff's Department, who had been called to assist at the crime scene, photographed the victim and the surrounding area. He made various measurements of the location of the victim in the alley in reference to the nearby house and jotted down notes on the position and appearance of the body.

An assistant from the Medical Examiner's Office made a cursory inspection of the victim, noting what appeared to be stab wounds in the throat and ligature marks on the neck, which suggested the boy also had been strangled.

After the evidence technicians finished, the small body was loaded into a waiting ambulance and taken to the county morgue, where an autopsy would be done as soon as possible.

Meanwhile, the officers spread out, searching for a

possible weapon and other evidence. As a result of the autopsy on Debra Evans completed that morning in Wheaton, the searchers also were looking for the fetus that was missing from the ripped-open mother.

When Scott had last seen Annette Williams about noon, she was carrying a newborn baby that she claimed to have given birth to the previous night. If the infant indeed was the one cut from Evans, the investigators wondered if Williams could have panicked after the killing of Joshua and abandoned the baby in the same area.

The searchers looked for the knife that had been described by Scott, but they did not find any possible weapon.

The uniformed officers and detectives also canvassed the neighborhood, seeking witnesses who might have seen or heard something, but came up with nothing. The residents in the house behind which the boy had been found were away from home during the time period that the slaying was thought to have happened.

Based on information gleaned from Patrice Scott, a pickup bulletin was issued for Annette Williams. Her address was unknown.

Maywood police had a photograph of Williams that had been taken in the past when she was handled on a minor offense.

She had lived in Maywood for a period of time, but she was not living at the old address now. Scott did not know Williams's present address, even though she had been there.

With the photo in hand, Van Stedum returned to the

Addison Police Department about 6:00 P.M. to pursue leads on Williams.

The DuPage County State Attorney's Office and the various law enforcement agencies in the county have a plan in place for cooperative major crime investigations. The agencies are furnished an assistant state attorney to work alongside the investigators from the beginning.

ASA Tom Epach joined the Addison detectives, to be available for legal direction. Filled in on the rapid developments by the information from Scott and Pruitt, Epach obtained an arrest warrant for Jacqueline Annette Williams on a charge of aggravated kidnapping in the abduction of Joshua Evans.

With the warrant and photograph of the suspect in their possession, the Addison, Maywood, Villa Park, and other area officers launched an all-out search.

It had been learned that Tina Martin—the woman whom Van Stedum and Simo contacted Friday morning in Wheaton while trying to locate Laverne Ward—was a sister of Annette Williams. The two detectives remembered that Williams's name had not come up during that brief talk with Martin.

After hearing Scott's story, Van Stedum phoned Martin and requested she come to the police station for another interview. She arrived shortly before 10:00 P.M. They did not talk for long.

Van Stedum asked if Martin could direct officers to where Williams now lived. Although she did not know the address, she said she might be able to take them there.

Van Stedum, Martin, and Epach were in one police

car, followed by other officers to assist in the arrest if the suspect was found at home. Among the lawmen was Lieutenant Jenkins. He had been conferring with the Addison investigators since Joshua's body had been found in his department's jurisdiction.

Martin directed Van Stedum to drive to the area of Barrington Road and Golf Road. She said she thought she could find her sister's house from that location.

As they drove along, Martin gave the detectives and assistant state attorney more information about her sister.

About 3:30 A.M. on Friday, Martin had received a phone call from Williams saying that she had given birth to her baby. Williams had been telling her sister and mother, Marsha Martin, for several months that she was pregnant. They were unaware that Williams—who had gained a lot of weight—could not have another baby, or that Williams had confided to one female friend that she had had a tubal ligation after the birth of her third child. First, Williams had said her baby was due in August. When that month had passed with no birth taking place, Williams then had said it would be October or November 1995.

Family and friends took her at her word, and Martin had given a baby shower for Williams in August 1995.

Present at the shower were relatives and friends, including Laverne Ward and Williams's boyfriend, Fedell Caffey. Annette had received gifts such as baby clothing, a baby carrier, and other items needed by a mother-to-be. They had played "baby" games, Martin recalled.

Caffey was said to be the father of the expected

child, Martin said. If it was a boy, Williams already knew what they would name him: Fedell Caffey Jr.

When her sister had phoned early this morning, the startled Martin had turned on a light and looked at her Caller ID box. Williams was calling from the home of one of her female friends in Wheaton.

Martin said she expressed doubt that her sister was a new mother, even though Williams's boyfriend, Fedell Caffey, came on the phone and confirmed Annette's statement.

Martin had awakened her mother, and together they went to the friend's house from where Williams called.

To their amazement, Annette was holding a newborn infant in her arms, Martin told the detective. The baby was wearing a baby hat and had a blanket wrapped around it. After one look, the mother of Tina and Annette had not believed it was Annette's baby, either.

The doubting relatives left after a few minutes. Back home Martin's mother phoned area hospitals to check if her daughter Annette had given birth in the past twenty-four hours. The hospitals had no record of a birth to a mother by that name.

From Martin's story, it appeared that the infant torn from Debbie Evans's womb might be alive and in the hands of one of the persons that Joshua Evans identified to Patrice Scott as the killers of his mother.

When Martin located and pulled up at her sister's residence on Cardiff Court in Schaumburg, Van Stedum got out, leaving Epach with Martin in the car. The detective relayed to the other officers that there now were two other witnesses, in addition to Scott, that Annette Williams had a newborn infant in her possession: her sister and mother.

After a brief conference, the officers divided into two groups, covering both the front and back doors of the residence. Included in the contingent of lawmen were members of the Maywood Police Department, alerted by Lieutenant Jenkins.

Van Stedum was with the officers who went to the front entrance. One of them knocked on the door and it was opened by a young girl, who looked to be about ten years old.

"We want to talk to Annette Williams," the investigator said.

The girl asked calmly, "Do you have a warrant?"

The question coming from such an obviously young child took the policeman by surprise, but he replied, "As a matter of fact, we do."

The girl stepped back to admit the group of officers. Inside, five children were watching the movie *Natural Born Killers* on TV.

The officers made a quick room-by-room search for Williams and the missing baby. No one, other than the five children, was there. The girl who had answered the door identified herself as Williams's eleven-year-old daughter. She did not know when her mother would be back.

The investigators learned that three of the youngsters belonged to Williams, and the other two were visiting overnight for a sleep-over.

Thinking of the woman friend to whose home Williams apparently had taken a newborn baby earlier that morning—according to the account of her sister, Tina Martin—Van Stedum decided to head for that residence in Wheaton on the chance the suspect might be there.

Again, Martin was to direct them to the address, since she also was acquainted with the friend.

Before leaving the home of Williams and her boyfriend, Caffey, Van Stedum met with his supervisor, Sergeant Sommers, and brought him up to date on the developments.

The detective also asked the sergeant for additional Schaumburg units to back up the investigators who would remain inside the town house in case Williams should return.

Staying at the town house were Lieutenant Jenkins and Detective Valerie Thomas of the Maywood Police Department. They were joined soon by Schaumburg detectives Bill Morris and Mike Rizer.

Van Stedum told Sommers that he, along with ASA Epach and Tina Williams who were outside in his car, was going to Wheaton to check for Williams and the baby at the home from where she called her sister so many hours ago on this lengthy Friday.

They would not reach that destination, however, because of what happened next in Schaumburg.

EIGHT

Time passed slowly for the investigators posted in the town house. The reinforcements from the Schaumburg Police Department, Detectives Bill Morris and Mike Rizer, had joined Jenkins and Thomas in their vigil.

The children were quiet. It was about 11:45 P.M. when the waiting officers heard the automatic garage door going up. The garage was in the basement level, near a stairway that went up to the second-level living quarters, where the detectives were.

Looking out, Jenkins saw a woman carrying an infant in a baby carrier coming up the stairs from the garage. He recognized Jacqueline Annette Williams from her photograph. He stepped out as she reached the stairway landing and confronted the startled woman.

"I'm a police officer and I have a warrant for your arrest." As he spoke, Jenkins reached out and took the baby carrier from her arms.

"That's my baby!" Williams cried.

Jenkins sat the baby carrier on the floor and instructed Detective Thomas to search Williams for possible weapons. None was found.

Meanwhile, Morris, also watching the stairs, saw a

man walk through the garage service door into the adjoining basement area. He was a thin-faced man with a mustache. He had on a pair of sweatpants and a yellow and white winter college jacket. He was carrying a baby car seat.

Morris dashed down the stairs. Shouting he was a police officer, he ordered the man, "Put your hands up!" The man complied, and when the detective asked his name, he said, "Fedell Caffey." No weapon was found on Caffey.

Leaving Williams in the custody of Thomas, Jenkins went down the stairs to check out the area for any other persons. He made a quick search of the rest of the garage and looked in the four-door gray car in which the suspects had arrived to make sure there was no one else.

Upstairs again, Jenkins heard Williams tell her daughter who had answered the door to "take care of your brother," referring to the baby in the carrier.

Jenkins informed the suspect that the girl could not do that and arrangements would be made for relatives to come get the five children.

Williams replied tartly, "That's my son. He was born last night at a friend's house. His name is Fedell Caffey Jr. I went to the hospital after he was born, and I got a birth certificate for him. I got it right here."

None of the investigators tried to question Williams at this time. A phone call was made on a cell phone to Detective Van Stedum, advising him that Williams and Caffey were in custody, and the missing baby, alive and seemingly well, had been with them.

It was 11:55 P.M. when Van Stedum received the welcome news. He wheeled the car around and headed back. Luckily, he had not gone far toward Wheaton.

He knew another long day lay ahead.

Arriving at the town house, Van Stedum asked an officer to stay with Martin, and the detective and Epach entered the front ground-level entrance. The first thing Van Stedum saw was the handcuffed Caffey sitting on the stairs under guard of a Schaumburg officer. He noticed Caffey was wearing a yellow or mustard-colored Grambling State University Tigers jacket. The detective did not know then the jacket would be of particular significance. Later it was discovered Caffey had a stash of crack cocaine and about $800 in cash concealed in his socks.

Van Stedum saw that the door leading to the garage area was open, and so was a door of a gray Mercury Sable parked there. He looked inside the car. There was what appeared to be a large bloodstain on the backseat floor carpeting, behind the driver's seat, and also on the back floor hump. At a glance it looked like someone had tried to remove the bloodstain. The dark reddish-brown splotch had what appeared to be wipe marks on it.

Epach had proceeded him upstairs. When Van Stedum entered the living room, he saw Epach and Detectives Dee Dee Ripsky and Thomas standing next to a table on which lay the infant taken from Williams. The baby was being undressed for examination. He had a healthy cry.

The clothing on the baby was open, exposing two large horizontal strips of tape holding a bloody piece of gauze in place over the navel area. The room was poorly lit, so Van Stedum held his flashlight on the infant as he was examined.

After looking at the baby, Van Stedum made arrangements for the infant to be taken for medical attention. He phoned the hospital to advise that the newborn infant was on his way there. He also contacted Detective Lullo at the Addison Police Department and told him to meet the ambulance bringing the baby.

This done, paramedic Dave Grant, accompanied by Detective Ripsky, took the baby in an ambulance to Alexian Brothers Medical Center in Hilton Grove Village.

Acting on the instructions of Sergeant Birk Christiensen of the Schaumburg Police Department, Detective Morris took the five children to the Schaumburg Police Station. They were to be picked up there by a relative who had been reached by telephone.

Lullo arrived at 12:51 A.M., about the same time as the ambulance. Detective Ripsky was holding the baby and turned him over to nurse Lisa Kaaperra.

Lullo took photographs of the infant, one of them a close-up of the navel area.

Medics who examined the infant pronounced him to be in excellent condition.

At the town house, Van Stedum introduced himself and Epach and told the suspect he would like to talk to her. But first he needed to read the Miranda warning card, which sets forth a suspect's legal rights.

As he read the rights one by one, Van Stedum asked

her if she understood each one. She replied she did and agreed to talk to the detective and Epach.

"Is that your baby?" the detective asked, referring to the infant she had in her arms when arrested.

"I just gave birth," Williams said. "His name is Fedell Caffey Jr."

Van Stedum asked if the handcuffed man downstairs was Caffey. Williams said yes and that she lived in the town house with Caffey. The detective asked if the officers could look around the town house and in the car parked in the garage. She gave her permission.

Detective Thomas left temporarily to attend to another assignment at the scene—the orderly parking of police cars that officers had exited hurriedly when arriving. When she returned to the town house, Williams now was seated on a bed in the north bedroom. Two officers were nearby.

Thomas sat down on the bed with the suspect, and the other officers left.

Over the next forty minutes at intervals, the handcuffed Williams talked to Thomas about the baby and when it was born. She claimed that she had given birth to the infant at the home of her girlfriend Betty Larson, who lived in Wheaton.

Williams said she had been given a shot of Demerol, and when she woke up at about 8:30 P.M. on Thursday, November 16, her friend told her that she had given birth to the baby. Following the birth, she took some Tylenol for the pain, she said.

Later, Williams, Larson, and the baby had left in the

girlfriend's car to see a doctor. But Larson had received a page and had to make a phone call, and they apparently had never gotten to the doctor.

Detective Thomas interrupted to ask Williams if she really believed that she had given birth to the baby.

Yes, she believed it, Williams answered, explaining that she had been to the doctor about seven months earlier, had a pregnancy test that turned out positive, but had never returned to the doctor after that.

Van Stedum, Epach, and the other investigators searched through the house.

They discovered two document-looking papers lying on the counter in the kitchen. One was a newborn physical discharge information sheet with the name of Fedell R. Williams Caffey on it.

The date of birth was shown as November 16, 1995. Date of discharge, the same. Birth weight, 5.6 pounds. Discharge weight, 5.3 pounds. Length, 19 inches. Head circumference, 34.5 inches. Card blood results: Type RH A positive. Significant history and findings: Healthy newborn male. Follow-up with Wheaton Medical Clinic.

There was a blue bow attached to the official-appearing document.

The other piece of paper bore the heading BIRTH CERTIFICATE. Below these large fancy-type words was a bracketed space with the instructions PLACE PHOTO HERE. The certificate read:

"This certifies that Fedell Raashaun Williams/Caffey was born to Jacqueline A. Williams in Central

DuPage Hospital at 8 P.M. on the 16th day of November 1995. Weight 5,3. Length, 19 inches."

In very fine print in the bottom left corner after a
tiny asterisk similar to one barely noticeable at the top
after the word "Certificate" was the short sentence:

"Not A Legal Birth Certificate."

In the right bottom corner in slightly larger script
type were the words:

"In Witness Whereof said Hospital certifies that
this Baby is Beautiful, uniquely wonderful, and
will become an outstanding individual."

An item among various dishes and eating utensils in
the dishwasher tray caught Van Stedum's attention. It
was an old-looking large, brown, rusty knife situated
blade up in the tray. It appeared that the dishwasher
had been run recently; all the things in the tray were
clean.

But the knife that stood out among the other items
looked more like it belonged in the garage instead of
a dishwasher, the detective thought. It matched the description given earlier by Patrice Scott of the weapon
used to stab Joshua Evans.

Van Stedum did not collect the knife, leaving it until
photographs could be made by evidence technicians
who would soon be there to process the scene.

Continuing the walk-through of the town house, the
investigators went up to the third level, where they no-

ticed baby-related items in a closet: Some baby clothes
hung there and a yellow bottle of Baby Magic was sitting on a shelf. The bottle especially drew their attention.

It looked like there was a blood spot on the bottle.

Before leaving to take Annette Williams back to
headquarters in Addison for questioning, Van Stedum
made arrangements for the gray Mercury Sable in the
garage to be towed to the police garage in Addison,
where it would be photographed and gone over thoroughly by fingerprint and forensic evidence technicians.

Caffey would be taken there in another police unit.
The detectives and assistant state attorney knew that
Caffey was a streetwise and hardened lawbreaker who
had long made his way dealing crack and other drugs.
They believed that Williams would be more likely to
talk.

All Caffey had to say was he didn't know nothing,
didn't know why he had been busted, didn't know that
being the daddy of a new baby boy was against the
law.

Van Stedum and Epach drove Williams to Addison.
They left the Schaumburg town house a few minutes
before 2:00 A.M. Saturday.

Williams was escorted into the office of Sergeant
Sommers and was seated. An officer was assigned to
watch her.

Through the hours ahead, she would give several versions of the tragic events surrounding the newly born
baby that she stubbornly claimed was hers.

NINE

During the early morning hours of Saturday, November 18, Detectives Van Stedum and Thomas and Lieutenant Jenkins talked with Williams at various intervals, and she told a hodgepodge of stories of how she came to be in possession of the infant.

Epach and Thomas were interviewing her together at about 5:20 A.M. on Saturday. Thomas, whom Williams seemed to relate to better than other investigators, did most of the talking with her.

"Do you know what happened Thursday night?" Thomas asked.

"I don't know anything about what happened," Williams replied.

But during an hour-and-a-half session of quiet questioning, she came up with several scenarios.

Williams blamed everything on Caffey and Ward. She claimed the two men gave the baby to Betty Larson, and Larson gave it to her, telling Williams that she had given birth at Betty's apartment after being in labor for two days while under the influence of two Demerol shots.

Caffey and Ward were together between 6:30 P.M. and 7:00 P.M. on Thursday, the day of the murders of Debra and Samantha. "They dropped me off at Betty's and said they were going to talk to Debbie about the unborn baby," Williams said.

Caffey later brought Joshua Evans to their house. The boy had been saying, "They hurt my mommy!" and Caffey told the boy he didn't know what he was talking about, Williams told the detective.

Sometime Thursday afternoon or evening, Williams and Larson met Caffey and Ward at a gas station, and the men told the women to meet them later in the parking lot where Evans lived. Williams said Ward told her that he was going to teach Debbie a lesson.

When the women arrived at the parking lot, Caffey and Ward came out of the apartment building and Joshua was behind them. Caffey was carrying the baby. Williams said Ward yelled at the boy to "get in the goddamned car!"

Williams said she never went into Evans's apartment, and she learned later that Evans had been shot and went into labor.

Williams also accused Patrice Scott of doing the things to Joshua that Scott in her statement to Villa Park officers had blamed on Williams. The investigators believed Scott was telling the truth, though she initially held back on some facts because of the fear instilled in her by Caffey's threats to kill her and her children if she told what happened.

According to Williams, she and Scott left Scott's apartment in Villa Park Friday morning to go to Schaumburg for Williams to show off her newborn infant. Scott gave the boy Visine and some soda pop.

Joshua stayed in the car sleeping for two hours after they arrived at Williams's town house, she said.

When they were leaving the town house and Caffey came to the car, Joshua got scared, said Williams. She related how Scott wanted to take the boy to the projects and drop him off, but Williams wanted to take him to a police station and leave him.

Williams's account was a complete reversal of the roles of the two women, as contrasted to Scott's statements about the horrible happenings in the Schaumburg town house and the Mercury Sable in which they drove to Maywood.

Williams stated Caffey first choked the boy with his hands, then put a cord around his neck and ordered the two women to pull on the ends to strangle him. Later in the car Williams was sitting in front, beside Scott who was driving, and Joshua and Caffey were in the backseat, Williams said. The suspect claimed Scott told her that Caffey had a knife and was stabbing Joshua.

Joshua was wrapped in a green sheet, Williams said, and Caffey took the sheet off when the boy was removed from the car in Maywood. Williams added that Scott threw out the sheet in an area near a large piano factory in the town of Bellwood.

Detective Thomas made notes on the interview, which she later included in her police reports, but the Williams story was so far-out that it was not typed up as a formal statement.

The horrible ordeal of Joshua Evans came to light fully when an autopsy was conducted on Saturday by

Dr. Joseph Lawrence Cogan, an assistant medical examiner for the Cook County Medical Examiner's Office.

Cogan's initial examination of the small body on the autopsy table disclosed that the boy had neck and head injuries. His face and head were red from the neck upward. Tiny pinpoint hemorrhages were visible on his face and ears. The hemorrhages, or broken blood vessels, began just above ligature marks on the neck.

The ruptured capillaries and small veins were suggestive of strangulation to the pathologist. Marks inflicted by the edges of some kind of ligature, such as a cord, were visible on the neck and indicated that the ligature had been wrapped twice around.

Other injuries included two large and deep stab wounds at the base of the neck just above the collarbone that went into the left part of his chest and penetrated the left carotid artery.

Some smaller cuts around the deeper stab wounds indicated the knife wielder might have first had trouble pushing the knife into the chest cavity, indicative of the weapon having a dull blade, in the pathologist's opinion.

As the pathologist put it, the edges of the wounds at that location "didn't look like the best stab wounds I've seen. . . . The edges were not nice and clean and the wounds inside the body were ragged, so they weren't really great, sharp stab wounds."

The two deeper wounds had gone all the way through the chest into the spinal area.

In the opinion of the pathologist, Joshua Evans was alive when stabbed and he aspirated the contents of his stomach into one lung that was not punctured. The lung lining had started to deteriorate from the gastric contents that included iodine.

As the pathologist explained, "Death could not have been instantaneous because one lung was collapsed, the chest cavity was filling with blood, and it would still take several minutes for the blood to fill the chest cavity. The child was very young and healthy, so it would take several minutes . . . [for death to occur]."

The doctor said he would be surprised "if the individual was still alive after thirty minutes without medical aid."

The pathologist ruled the cause of death was from multiple injuries: strangulation, stab wounds, and the aspiration of the gastric contents into the lung.

Joshua had died a torturous, unimaginably painful death.

A search warrant seeking the various items the investigators had seen during the walk-through of the town house before taking Williams to the Addison Police Department, was issued and executed at the Cardiff address at 3:25 A.M.. on Saturday by Addison detective Paul Hardt. Also there to work the search with him was Detective Joe Lullo.

The detectives took over the secured crime scene from Detective Bill Cooley of the Wheaton Police Department.

Before beginning the search, Hardt photographed the various rooms, showing items that subsequently would be collected as evidence.

Hardt took pictures of an infant carrier on the floor

near the kitchen table; the open silverware tray in the dishwasher that contained a wooden-handle butcher knife with a rusty blade placed blade up in the tray; a bedsheet on a closet shelf; a blue baby bouncer on the floor of a walk-in closet in the master bedroom; several items of baby clothing hanging in the same closet; numerous baby items on a top shelf, including a baby starter set and bottles of Baby Magic lotion.

One yellow bottle of baby lotion bore reddish stains that looked like blood; some baby bottle formulas and baby blankets also were spotted.

Detective Hardt also took pictures of black plastic garbage bags and tan-colored paper grocery sacks on the floor of the garage along one wall just inside the entrance doorway from the foyer. After the pictures were snapped, Detective Lullo, Hardt, and other detectives began the distasteful job of opening the bags and carefully sorting through the stuff inside that was poured on the garage floor.

In one of the grocery sacks that had the words "Thank you, Thank you" on it, the detectives found a used baby diaper.

Among the garbage litter the detectives discovered a white cable cord similar to one that would be used for a VCR or computer hookup. The cord had a spot on it that looked like blood.

Hardt also took pictures in the basement laundry room, which was furnished with a black metal daybed. Items of clothing were scattered over the floor. The detectives sorting though the clothing located a tan and maroon-colored scarf with African symbols or markings on it.

From Patrice Scott and Williams, it had been learned that such a scarf had been tied around Joshua Evans's mouth by Fedell Caffey to keep him quiet while he was seated on the daybed.

The investigators completed the search authorized by the warrant shortly after 5:00 A.M.

They did not immediately collect some of the evidence discovered, preferring to obtain a second search warrant that would specify particular items to be taken as evidence.

Hardt executed that warrant Saturday afternoon. The rusty-blade knife, the white cord in the laundry room, and the scarf were among other items taken as possible evidence.

Hardt later turned over the knife to Detective Van Stedum, who showed it to Williams during her interrogation.

On Saturday afternoon Annette Williams broke down. She began to cry, put her arms down on the table, put her head down, and sobbed, "I was there. I will tell the truth."

Present also when Williams volunteered to make a confession were Detectives Van Stedum and Colin C. Simpson.

The statement, which Williams dictated to ASA Epach, was recorded in his handwriting. It was taken after the suspect's legal rights were read to her.

Each of the seven pages was signed by Williams and the state attorney and detectives.

It was completed at 6:00 P.M.

TEN

The statement read:

"My name is Jacqueline Annette Williams. I am 28 years old. I live at [ ] Cardiff Court in Schaumburg, Ill. I live there with my boyfriend, Fedell Caffey, who is age 22.

"We have been together about two years, and we have lived at this address since March or April [1995]. Everyone calls me Annette.

"I have been given each of the above rights [listed on the first page of the statement] and understand each of them. I am making this statement of my own free will and because it is the truth.

"For our entire relationship together, my boyfriend Fedell has been trying to get me pregnant so that he could have a baby boy. For the longest time he has told me he has 2 requirements for our child together—that we have a boy and that it be light-skinned so that it resembles him.

"I got pregnant, but had an abortion and a miscarriage. Over the course of the last four months I have become aware of the fact that Laverne Ward, who is called Verne, has been upset with Debra

Evans, who is the mother of his 2-year-old son named Jordan.

"Last Thursday, Nov. 16, 1995, Laverne, Fedell and myself, decided to go by Debbie Evans's house. Fedell drove us over in our gray Sable. Verne said he was going to talk to Debbie about Jordan and the arguments they were having.

"Debbie lived at [   ] Swift Road, Apt. [   ], in Addison. She lived there with her children,— Samantha, age 10; Joshua, age 8; and Jordan, age 2. She was also 9 months pregnant, and was due to deliver on Monday after checking into the hospital on Sunday.

"We arrived there at about 9 P.M. and the kids were still up. We rang the buzzer and Debbie buzzed us in. Once inside the apartment we all sat down and Debbie sat on a small couch across from the TV.

"We were having a conversation about my daughter Christina's birthday party on Friday, and I got up to go to the bathroom. I went in and heard a loud banging noise, and then I walked out of the bathroom and saw Debbie laying on her back in front of the couch. She was blowing small bubbles out of her mouth and her eyes were blinking open and closing rapidly.

"I saw Fedell with the gun, which was a small, silver-colored automatic. Verne was [at] the side of her by her neck and appeared to be stabbing her.

"Fedell then put the gun up in his waistband and then he took a knife and started cutting her stomach open. He was cutting crossway across her abdomen at first, and I could see yellow fat.

"Then as he cut more I saw the head of the baby sticking out. I wanted that baby and Fedell knew it was a boy. Debbie had already known and had chose a name, Elijah, for the boy—so he wanted it, too. He continued to cut it out of her abdomen and the baby began to emerge.

"It had no color and was covered with blood and mucous. Fedell began to pull the baby out and I was right at his side. The baby looked limp and I thought it looked lifeless. Fedell took his knife and cut the baby's cord.

"The knife is shown in a picture the state's attorney showed me. Fedell at that point didn't want the baby anymore—he thought he killed it.

"I still wanted it, so I grabbed it and he was limp. I blowed in his nose and he started coughing. I saw bubbles and I put him down and blowed in his mouth. During all this, Jordan, the 2-year-old, was right on the coffee table. The older 2 children were in the bedroom.

"As I finished with the baby I put a hat on him and a sleeper. I then saw Fedell and Verne go back to the bedroom where the children Joshua and Samantha were. I grabbed a blanket and Joshua came running up crying that Verne and Fedell were in the bedroom hurting Samantha.

"He asked 'Where is my mommy?' I had put a blanket over her and her exposed belly and covered her up. I told him not to touch.

"Then he vomited and ran to the bathroom. I

picked up the baby and started carrying him out when Joshua grabbed my leg and said he didn't want to stay there. Joshua had grabbed his green coat and boots but had on no pants. He said Verne and Fedell were bad and me and him went out the back.

"Joshua started screaming, 'What are we going to do?'

"He waited out back and then walked out front and met with Fedell and Verne. We all got in the car, including my baby and Joshua, and drove until we dropped Verne off on Roosevelt.

"We then drove to Patrice's home and dropped Joshua off. I lied and told her Joshua's mom had been shot at a drug spot and she needed to watch the boy for me. I told him I would be back in the morning.

"Fedell drove to get some SMA and pampers. We went to the 7-11 and got baby wipes. Before this we had driven out to Betty's who had bandaged the belly button because it was cut too short.

"My mom and my sister Tina came to Betty's and Fedell told them I had had my baby that night. My mother said, 'No, you didn't and saw the color of the baby and asked to see some papers. I got some phony documents the next day. . . .

"We then went home for the night. We washed off some blood—some from the baby squirting blood on the coat, the gold-and-white one he [Fedell] stole from the murder scene. I saw there was blood on it.

"On Friday morning I left the house at 10 to 7,

dropped my kids off at school and went to Patrice's house to pick up Joshua at 8:30 A.M. or there abouts.

"I went inside and found out that Joshua had told Patrice all about the murders. I knew at that point we were in deep trouble. I took Joshua from the house and took him to Schaumburg.

"He still had no pants on and Verne and Fedell were at the house. Patrice had come along because I told her I had just given birth and wanted her to see the baby.

"Fedell told me to tie a scarf around his [Joshua's] mouth. I did but then untied [it]. We were all afraid because Joshua knew what had happened and could identify us. Then Verne left.

"At that point I asked him [Joshua] to sit on the bed. Fedell had a piece of a scarf and that's what I used to tie around his head with the knot behind his head.

"Fedell asked me to get a knife upstairs and I did. I then returned and gave Fedell the knife. Joshua was screaming and frightened to death. Patrice was also frightened because Fedell was yelling threats at her.

"We then decided to get Joshua into the car. Joshua was put on the floor in the back behind the driver. Fedell was on the backseat and I was in the driver's seat. Fedell wrapped a cord around Joshua's neck several times and then Fedell had me pull on one end of the rope. He ordered Patrice to hold on to the other end.

"Joshua was hysterical, crying, sobbing, and

moaning. We dropped the rope and Fedell began stabbing the boy. I started to drive to the city of Maywood to dump the body. I used to live in Maywood, and I pulled into an alley that is a 'T' with an adjacent fence. We stopped.

"Joshua was wrapped in a sheet and I grabbed the sheet and he was set outside the car. I got back in and dumped the sheet at the piano company.

"I then drove to Patrice's and dropped her off.

"Joshua was killed because he knew who did the murders. Fedell and I were arrested later that same night. I gave the police consent to search my house and my car and was present when Fedell gave consent as well.

"I have been treated well by the police and prosecutor. No promises or threats have been made to me.

"I am dictating this statement to Assistant State Attorney Thomas Epach who is writing it down as I tell him. I have reviewed this statement and it is true and accurate.

"I have signed each page after reading it because it is true. I have been given the chance to tape record or video tape this statement but do not wish to. Also at the conclusion I identified the knife used to kill Joshua."

Early Saturday evening Detective Cathy Vrchota of the Addison investigation unit was assigned to go to Patrice Scott's apartment in Villa Park to search for the iodine bottle that was thought to have been discarded by Williams after giving a dose to Joshua Evans.

The detective had been instructed to look for the bottle in the garbage. She went to a garbage pile beside the apartment building. Rummaging in the garbage, she removed some napkins and discovered the brown iodine bottle near the top of the refuse.

She placed it in an evidence bag and later put it in the evidence locker room at the police station.

Acting on the information from Williams, Lieutenant Jenkins drove to Bellwood late Saturday night to search for the sheet in which Joshua was wrapped before his body was dumped.

He concentrated his efforts in the area of 25th Avenue and Harrison Street, near a large piano factory. Finally he found the sheet lying on the north side of Harrison Street in the 2800 block.

Jenkins observed that the sheet had been discarded less than a half block from the entrance to the Eisenhower Expressway, which was along the route taken by Annette Williams when driving to Maywood to get rid of Joshua's body that was wrapped in the sheet.

Jenkins called the Cook County Sheriff's Department criminalistic unit to photograph and take custody of the sheet, since the location was in the Cook County jurisdiction. He had the photographer shoot another picture that showed the sheet's location in relation to the Eisenhower Expressway ramp sign.

The investigators had an idea that might link the recovered sheet to Annette Williams even better than the part of her confessions that told about the sheet wrapped around Joshua being thrown out of the car.

Detective Thomas was assigned to look for possible similar sheets in Williams's town house.

Any woman knows that if there is one sheet in hand, it has a matching mate somewhere. Detective Thomas looked in the logical places and found the matching sheet in a bedroom. She also came across a matching pillowcase on a shelf in a second-floor closet.

The discoveries neatly tied up the incriminating sheet evidence against Joshua Evans's killers.

ELEVEN

Murder is an exacting science to a particular breed of police investigator—the evidence technician. The evidence tech is never glamorized much in television mystery shows or books. The homicide detective is the one in the spotlight.

The evidence tech deals in bloodstains and other body fluids; in measuring distances and making videotapes and still photographs and diagrams; in fingerprints and footprints and body hair; and in recording and preserving such things for analysis in the crime lab.

The tech is the one who takes swab samples from bloodstains; lifts latent fingerprints by using special techniques and materials; examines dead bodies and stained clothing; sifts through debris and trash and garbage with a technical eye out for something like a clue.

It is the scientifically trained techs on the scene and in the lab that draw the final conclusions from homicide's litter: the bloodstains, blood spatters and blood spray patterns, the semen and saliva stains, the latent fingerprints and the useless smudges, the broken glass or wood splinters from a smashed window or a kicked-in door.

In the big-word circles, police evidence techs are called criminal forensic experts.

How well these specialists do their jobs means the difference between ultimately putting the pieces of a homicide puzzle together or not, ultimately nailing a perpetrator or not.

Among other job challenges facing an evidence tech is that savvy criminal defense lawyers always come down hard on forensic and fingerprint testimony from the witness chair. Defense lawyers work at confusing the technical conclusions that forensic techs lay out for juries.

An evidence tech goes through exhaustive training and the continuing education afforded by updating seminars given by the FBI and state law enforcement agencies.

One of the Addison Police Department evidence techs summoned from his residence by phone to North Swift Road on that early, cold morning of November 17, 1995, was officer Barry Muniz.

From the time he received the call and was given the address, Muniz found himself in a state of déjà vu. Not quite a decade ago, he had responded to a homicide call at this same apartment in this same room with an eerily similar murder victim mutilated on the floor.

Lillian LaCrosse had been the young mother of three small children, found by her husband when he returned from his night shift job the next morning.

Muniz clearly remembered following a trail of blood

from the LaCrosse apartment to another nearby apartment building where the killer was arrested.

Muniz back then theorized the killer had a snack and took a bath after his crime because there was blood on his refrigerator and his bathtub. Technical evidence sometimes can tell what happened better than eyewitnesses.

That murderer was still on the Illinois death row. His appeal recourses through both the state and the federal appellate systems had not been exhausted, so no execution date had been set.

Now Muniz began his investigation of the second murder that had happened in the same apartment. And again, as ten years earlier, it seemed like blood was everywhere.

When Muniz arrived at the murder scene about 3:30 A.M., he met with another evidence technician already there: John Klco, an eighteen-year-veteran officer who had worked hundreds of crime scenes during his career. Klco had been on routine patrol when he heard an officer, who was on a call, advise the dispatcher that he possibly had a homicide.

Klco notified the dispatcher that he would be en route to the apparent slaying scene.

The first patrol officer to arrive was standing near a distressed-looking man identified as James Edwards, who was sitting on the inside stairway and holding a small boy clad in a long red sleeper. The child was the only known survivor of the carnage inside, Klco learned.

Hearing that another small boy was missing from the apartment, Klco, along with Sergeant Paul Hofferage, went inside to search. There was speculation the boy might have been killed also and concealed some place in the apartment. Or he might have been so frightened that he still was hiding somewhere.

They looked in every room, underneath clothing, the furniture, in closets, but failed to find the boy.

Also present was another evidence tech, James Kaplan, as well as Detectives Mark Van Stedum and Mike Simo, who subsequently would be assigned as the lead detectives in the case.

Several patrol units were there—the uniform officers now spread over the grounds looking in Dumpsters and shrubbery, any place that might conceal a body or some evidence.

Muniz paired with Klco to make a videotape of all the rooms before any work started to collect biological and physical evidence. The two technicians did a quick walk-through of the apartment before beginning to put it on film.

They wanted to locate possible evidence so they would not accidentally destroy it. They wanted to get a general feeling for the layout.

Muniz saw a woman prone and faceup on the living room floor and a young girl in a back bedroom, both of them savaged by knife wounds and saturated with blood.

Muniz was told the woman's stomach had been slashed wide open, in addition to other sharp instrument wounds. The once pretty young girl, so pitiful a sight with the brutish stab wounds she had suffered, lay on her back on a sleeping pallet in the bedroom.

Klco told Muniz the victims were Debra Evans and

her young daughter, Samantha. He added that the girl's seven-year-old brother, Joshua, was missing and it was not known if he was dead or alive.

After completing the videotape, Klco and Muniz took numerous still photographs of the bodies and bloodstains in the living room, hallway, bathroom, and two bedrooms; they also photographed the kitchen area that showed a cabinet drawer next to the kitchen stove pulled out and a silverware tray from the drawer on the counter.

In the bathroom the vanity, sink, and wall were splattered with blood and there was blood on the floor. Blood had spattered on a tube of toothpaste on the vanity counter. The technicians also noticed what appeared to be a child's bloody footprint on the floor.

Later, investigators would link the tiny impression in blood to little Jordan Evans, the tyke who had wandered aimlessly in the bloody apartment until James Edwards found him bloodstained and sobbing.

Moving to the master bedroom, the techs photographed a bloodstained Ace bandage found on one corner of the bed, and bloodstains that had soaked through the covers and sheets and into one corner of the mattress.

In the smaller bedroom a piece of green paper on the floor beside Samantha's body was photographed. What looked like bloody fingerprints were apparent on the paper.

Checking the back stairway, the techs spotted a blue and red cap with a Flintstone cartoon character on it. The cap later was identified as one that Samantha had outgrown and given to Joshua. It apparently had been dropped when the boy fled down the stairs.

There was a spot of blood on a stair step close to the cap.

After the photographs were taken, the evidence officers split into two teams to examine and take samples if possible from the bloodstains and to dust for fingerprints in every room. Klco and Officer Russ Schecht would seek fingerprints from surfaces in the apartment. Muniz and Kaplan would take swab samples from the bloodstains to be submitted to the crime lab for analysis and typing.

The evidence technicians donned sterile rubber gloves to avoid contaminating any evidence. If the gloves got soiled as they worked, they would change to another pair.

If ever there was an appropriate saying for evidence techs, it well could be that old familiar one: "Blood will tell." Of course, it had a different meaning than the familiar notation. In a murder investigation blood will help tell what happened.

For example, whether bloodstains are left in splatters or in spurts has different interpretations to those trained in analyzing blood patterns, a science in itself.

The blood work was a two-man operation: Muniz removed a new swab from a previously sealed package—a long Q-Tip-type handle with a piece of cotton on the end—used an eyedropper to apply a couple of drops from a sterile water container to the cotton, and handed it to Kaplan.

Kaplan dipped the swab into a bloodstain, then broke off part of the handle and dropped the cotton sample into a sterile plastic vial readied by Muniz. The sample was labeled with the time and the location where it was taken and initialed by the officer.

Such detailed procedure is vital to maintaining the "chain of evidence" when a case comes to trial—meaning it must be proven that evidence is in the same condition and preserved as when it was found at a scene.

Muniz and Kaplan took bloodstain samples from the living room, hall, bathroom, bedrooms, and kitchen.

Meanwhile, Klco and Schecht dusted for fingerprints and collected physical evidence throughout the apartment. Klco was examining the love seat next to which Debra Evans's body was sprawled when he discovered a shell casing behind the love seat; the shell was on the floor, next to the baseboard of the wall.

The casing appeared to be a .25-caliber cartridge. The bullet would be recovered later from the woman's head during the autopsy.

Klco and Schecht had a specific plan to make sure that all surfaces were covered during the hunt for prints. They would meet in the center of a room, divide the room from the center, and work outward in a clockwise circle.

The smoother a surface, the better the chance of getting a fingerprint. The selected surfaces were dusted with black fingerprint powder, and if a latent print was visible, latent fingerprint tape was pressed over the print to lift and then place it on a fingerprint card.

Some of the latent prints were photographed without trying to lift them on tape.

The last thing the technicians did about midafternoon

before closing and securing the apartment was to try another method to reveal latent prints on porous surfaces on which the fingerprint powder would not be effective.

Klco and Schecht first made certain that the apartment was shut up—all windows and doors closed tightly. They then set small plates of Super Glue in every room. One of the body secretions in sweat is an amino acid, which would be present in latent fingerprints on surfaces that could not be dusted with powder. The Super Glue fumes adhere to amino acids and make latent prints easier to find. The fumes also harden the prints that might be on an item and lessen the chance of accidentally destroying them.

Physical evidence removed from the apartment besides the shell casing and the bloodstained shears on the outside wall included the small love seat, patches of bloodied carpeting, the green piece of paper from Samantha's bedroom, the bloody Ace bandage, and the bedding stained with blood.

Before leaving the apartment that first afternoon, the investigators attached police department locks with large hinges on the doors, which also were secured with police tape. An around-the-clock police guard was left at the scene. The next day when the evidence men returned and opened up the apartment, they found about one hundred additional latent prints. All of the fingerprints and the bloodstain samples would be submitted to the DuPage County Crime Lab for comparison with blood samples and the fingerprints from any suspects, the victims, and anyone else who might have been in the apartment.

The evidence crew would spend three more days in their foot-by-foot scrutiny of the apartment interior for clues. The apartment would remain locked and under constant police guard through January 11, 1996, to finish the crime scene work.

Not until then would the apartment be released by the police for family members to remove personal items.

On Friday afternoon, Ray Rodriquez, a detective forensic specialist with the DuPage County Sheriff's Department, went to the county morgue and took a set of what is termed "major case" fingerprints from the body of Samantha Evans. He prepared fingerprint cards for both hands of the girl. Earlier, similar print cards had been made from the body of Debra Evans.

The victim prints would be used in the process of eliminating fingerprints found in the North Swift Road apartment.

Rodrique next went to the Addison Police Department garage to process the gray four-door Mercury Sable that Williams and Caffey had been in when arrested at the Schaumburg town house early that morning.

He went over both the exterior and interior of the vehicle with fingerprint powder. He recovered six latent prints from the outside of the car, but found none inside. In fact, the lack of any prints probably could be attributed to what obviously had been a thorough washing and scrubbing inside the car, in Rodriquez's opinion.

He found a large reddish-brown stain that he recognized as blood on the back floorboard, directly behind the driver's seat. He noticed what seemed to be wipe marks amid the bloodstain, lending credence to his belief that the stain and all of the interior had been scrubbed with some cleaning agent.

Nevertheless, he made "tapings"—pressing tape onto the bloodstain in hopes of lifting some trace evidence for examination under the lab microscopes. He photographed the large stain and then vacuumed the interior of the car using an evidence filter that might pick up hair or other trace evidence.

All this done, the evidence tech cut out a large portion of the bloodstained carpeting for lab scrutiny.

TWELVE

Even before Annette Williams gave her confession in which she said she, Caffey, and Ward had arrived at Debra Evans's apartment about 9:00 P.M., the detectives had a pretty good idea of when the murders had happened. The questioning of James Edwards and other apartment residents elicited information that fit with the time she had given.

When tenants of the North Swift Road apartments began getting up Thursday morning, the homicide detectives and uniformed officers divided up the several buildings in the sprawling complex and started knocking on doors seeking possible witnesses.

The canvassing of the apartments would continue over the next few days. Investigators wanted to make sure that someone who might know something would not be missed.

Early on, the door-to-door efforts yielded some results.

A woman occupant of an apartment in the same building where the killings happened recalled that she had heard a gunshot between 8:30 and 9:30 P.M. At the time she had been in her bedroom talking on the phone to a friend. The window in the room had been open.

"I heard a shot outside that sounded like it came from the north," she told an investigator. "I went out to see if anyone was hurt, but didn't see anything."

She had returned and resumed her phone conversation.

She estimated she had been on the phone about an hour, but she could not remember when she had heard the shot—at the beginning or toward the end of the conversation.

"I can't remember exactly," she said.

In the same building the officers talked to a woman who lived in an apartment below the Evans apartment. She had heard strange sounds from upstairs

"There was a very hard thump or thud that would have been on the floor of that apartment," she said.

She estimated the time in relation to the time she had gone to bed, which was 11:00 P.M. The thump she heard had been about an hour or so before that. She pointed out the spot on the ceiling where it sounded like the loud noise had come from. Later comparison showed that the spot the woman indicated was the location where Debra Evans had been shot and fallen to the living room floor.

The investigators found another neighbor woman in the apartment complex who had heard people talking in the front parking lot Thursday evening. When she had peered out a window, the woman had seen four people. One of them had been a man in a dark sweatshirt with a hood. He had approached the three others who were standing together and yelled, "I'm going to do something!"

"Then he lowered his voice," the witness said.

The woman had a good reason for being interested in what was going on in the parking lot. She recently had bought a new car, and she was a little nervous about the prospect of someone vandalizing or even stealing it—times being what they are, with stories every day about kids or adults swiping new cars or just damaging them for the fun of it.

So she had looked closely at the group huddled in the parking lot.

She recalled that one man was shorter than the others, and another man was much taller. One man appeared to be a "light-skinned African American or a Hispanic," the witness said.

It was known to investigators that Verne Ward was considerably on the short side—about five feet four inches tall. Caffey, they knew, was a light-skinned African American.

The woman said she did not see where the people went, whether they had weapons, or what they did next.

Debra Evans, Samantha, Joshua, and Jordan had regular times for going to bed. James Edwards was well acquainted with his family's nightly routine. Settled somewhat from the shock of finding the bodies, he mentioned some information that helped pinpoint the general time when the merciless killers had shown up.

The children usually were in bed by 8:00 P.M., especially Joshua and Samantha who had to get up early

for school. Samantha regularly wore her favorite Pocahontas nightgown, and Joshua, like boys his age often
do, slept in his shorts and a T-shirt.

Debra Evans, fully pregnant and going into the hospital
Sunday to have the birth induced, always was in bed by
9:00 or 10:00 P.M., in keeping with her expectant-mother
health routine.

When the murderers struck, Samantha and Josh were
wearing their sleeping garments. Debra had not yet
slipped into her sleeping attire. She still was dressed
in slacks and sweater and underclothing. She was barefoot, something she liked to be in the evening when
the day's chores were winding down.

Based on these descriptions by Edwards, it seemed
Williams's estimate that the murder suspects came to
the apartment about 9:00 P.M. was right in line—considering how the victims were dressed when Edwards
found them.

Edwards also was able to tell Detectives Van Stedum
and Simo that several items were missing from the
apartment and apparently had been taken by the intruders.

Missing were a yellow Grambling University winter
jacket Edwards had bought only recently, a jacket Caffey was wearing when arrested in Schaumburg the next
night. Also gone were some pants and shirts, Edwards
reported.

Some money that had been on a jewelry box on the
bedroom dresser was gone. Part of that cash had been
$20 that Debra had set aside to pay her sister for a
baby swing.

As he went through the apartment room by room

with the detectives to see what might have been disturbed or missing, Edwards noticed that a boom box with two attached speakers was gone.

The tape player belonged to Samantha. It had been given to her a few months earlier when the girl had visited her father and her grandmother in Florida. It was something that "Sam," as everybody affectionately called her, was extremely proud of.

This new information gave the detectives something definite to look for as they sought evidence against the suspected slayers.

If a detective is anything, he is a question asker. Especially homicide detectives, like Mark Van Stedum, Mike Simo, Paul Hardt, Dave Wall, Cathy Vrchota, and Joe Lullo, as well as Maywood detective Valerie Thomas.

The Addison Police Department was a small department as police departments go—maybe sixty-six officers, uniform and plain clothes, and thirty-five or so civilian employees. The investigations unit, with its seven or eight detectives, handled all types of crimes, major and minor.

When a major case came along, such as the Evans murders, every detective on the force was involved sooner or later, morning or night, and sometimes both.

Mike Simo was born and grew up in Chicago. He attended Southern Illinois University at Carbondale, Illinois, when he finished high school. He graduated from college with an associate degree in law enforcement.

He was hunting for a career, but didn't want to sit behind a desk. He certainly got his wish. First as a patrolman for nine years, starting in 1980, and then as a detective, he put in a lot of routine patrol hours and some occasional hairy ones when things livened up, as they will do even in a small and quiet village.

Little town or big town, a cop gets exposed to it all—especially the dangers and the risks that go with a uniform and badge.

Once in a while along comes the big case, the one that makes blazing headlines everywhere. The case that draws the spotlight that a nice quiet place such as Addison would just as soon avoid.

But murder happens, sometimes extremely bad murders, and all a detective can do is work his butt off and know that sooner or later, the break will come and the case will unravel.

One thing Detective Simo knew for certain—he did not spend much time sitting behind a desk.

Detective work is asking questions and more questions, double-checking the answers, and talking to anyone and everyone who might throw light on the subject. The detective talks to a victim's friends and family, and some biased and some unbiased witnesses.

In the end, if the detective is lucky, it all comes together, and then he or she can spend hours and hours in a courtroom, usually on their day off. Then it's the officer who is pounded with questions when he takes the witness stand.

But court time is usually a long way off when a big

murder case breaks. The homicide detective is going to work long hours and lose lots of sleep.

And if he has asked enough questions and gotten the right answers, in the end it's all worth it.

Van Stedum and Simo were in the seek-and-question stage. They talked to Debra Evans's grieving mother, Jacalyn, and also Wendy Jo Williams, a sister. (No relation to Annette Williams.) Questioning sorrowful family members is one of a detective's most dreaded duties in crime's tragedies.

They would interview Evans's friends, former friends, and ex-boyfriends later.

Anyone who had ever known Debra Evans, or had anything to do with her, would be visited by Van Stedum, Simo, and other investigators.

Asking for understanding for their intrusion at this time of deep grieving, the sleuths learned that Debra Evans's family was one rooted in Christian faith. It was a family sorrowful over the drifting away of a happy, church-attending young daughter such as Debra. She was a popular and bubbling girl in high school, a talented guitar player and singer of beautiful hymns.

Unexplainably, she had cut loose into a shadowy world of unhappiness. She gave birth out of wedlock. There were live-in boyfriends. Debbie found herself with some women friends living in the war zone of lawbreaking and loose living that is the growing American culture of drugs and violence and discarded morality.

One big plus for Debra—and her devoted relatives were thankful to the Lord for this—she never was a participant in the drug circles herself. She never used any, never dealt any. But, unfortunately, she at times lived with dominant men who were involved in drugs and often in violence. She had been a victim of domestic violence herself more than once. But in spite of it all, she seemed to go back to the source of her misery and give them another chance and even try to help them.

She was known as a person who always would help somebody in need, even as economically poor as she usually was.

She especially tried to help some of her female friends—women with the wrong men who were trying to live ordinary lives for their children's sake. They were women who loved their kids, took them to school and sports events, had birthday parties, had a mother's dream for their children, and endured the failings of the type of men to whom they seemed to gravitate.

Debra Evans's first love, Scott Gilbert, who was the father of Samantha, and James Edwards, a hardworking man with a regular job who was a good surrogate father to her children, probably were the best men ever to come into her troubled and relatively short life.

THIRTEEN

The downward spiral of Debra Evans—from a happy, church-centered lifestyle into the unstable existence she chose in the last few years before her death—puzzled her relatives and friends. Somebody compared Evans's metamorphosis to a flower in a garden slowly overrun by wild weeds that eventually wipe it out.

Plainly, she had been unable to cope with life in the fast lane.

Yet, even with her changed ways, she still was a woman with good intentions, always unselfish and more than willing to help out people down on their luck.

A friend who knew her in high school may have hit on the answer. Suffering from low self-esteem brought on by the demeaning events in her young life, she sought love and affection in the wrong places from the wrong kind of men.

Yet, in her last days, Evans was trying to return to the happy days. During the month before her murder, Evans had enrolled Samantha and Joshua in a youth program at a small Baptist church and attended the church services herself.

"She said she had gone here as a child," the minister recalled.

* * *

Debra Evans was a small-town girl, born in Keeney-ville, a hamlet in the Oak Park, Illinois, area. She was the oldest of five children; she had two sisters and two brothers. Her parents had married in 1966 in a Keeney-ville church. At the time of Debra's birth in 1967, her father was in the U.S. Army.

Her parents separated about 1989 and were divorced two years later. Sam Evans, Debra's father, and her youngest brother moved downstate; the rest of the children remained in Keeneyville with their mother, Jacalyn. At the time of the divorce, Jacalyn was working as a housecleaner and was on public aid.

Their mother was a devoted Christian woman who regularly took the children to church. But in her junior year at a high school in Roselle, Illinois, Debra began having increasing moods of independence, a new attitude that—though not uncommon to a teenager—would spell trouble. Even though she transferred to a Christian school in Wisconsin, her teenage restlessness continued and she gradually drifted away from her religious background and church friends.

She was seventeen years old and working part-time as a baby-sitter at a Carol Stream, Illinois, apartment complex in the summer of 1984 when she met sixteen-year-old Scott Gilbert. A year later, Debra gave birth to Gilbert's child, Samantha.

The two teenagers decided they were too young to get married. Over the years Gilbert never lost touch with his daughter and he remained a good friend to

Debra. When Gilbert married another woman, both Debra and Samantha were at the wedding.

He and Samantha visited frequently, and they talked regularly on the phone.

Two years after Samantha was born, Debra had another baby, Joshua. She never revealed the identity of the father. A close friend remembered that Debra "told me the second baby didn't have the same father as Samantha, and she was afraid they would take the baby away from her."

The year 1988 was a hard one for Debra Evans. During that period she had limited contact with her relatives. Before the birth of her son, Debra frequently went dancing at a local club. She loved dancing. It blended well with her musical interests.

But the places she went to dance put her in contact with the wrong type of men.

"It seemed that she would hang out with any man who offered a sort of love or affection that raised her low opinion of herself," said the close friend from their high school days.

While Evans was temporarily estranged from her parents, the former classmate had visited her and found that she was sleeping on the floor of her partially furnished apartment in Hanover Park because she could not afford a bed. The friend loaned her furniture and also offered to buy pictures to give the apartment a brighter look.

In the early 1990s, Evans met Laverne Ward, a short and cocky small-time lawbreaker. When they met, she was living on public aid. Ward became her live-in boy-friend. Debra's third child, Jordan, was born of this re-lationship.

Debra's feelings toward Ward understandably began to sour. He beat her up and sometimes locked her in their apartment. They argued and fought frequently. He was arrested once in 1993 on domestic violence charges and sentenced to two years' probation.

They separated, but she later let him return, though they soon would break up again. The "on-again, off-again" relationship, as friends described it, would be a pattern in Evans's life. Sometimes she let a female friend who was temporarily down on her luck share her apartment.

Poor as she was, she always would share with needy people. Ironically, Jacqueline Annette Williams had been one of those guests. Williams and her children lived with Evans and her children for about two months.

Scott Gilbert made a point of phoning his daughter Samantha twice a week, usually on Wednesday and Sunday. He would talk to Debra, too.

During the Christmas holidays in 1994, Samantha went to Tallahassee, Florida, to visit her father and his wife. Gilbert's mother gave Samantha a portable stereo with two attached speakers and earphones for Christmas. Samantha was proud of the boom box that she carried back home. The girl flew back to Illinois with Gilbert's sister and brother-in-law.

In the summer of 1995, when school was out, Gilbert

and his wife came to Illinois and picked up Samantha for a six-week visit. She brought her prized stereo with her.

At the end of the summer, the Gilberts flew back with Samantha. Gilbert drove her to the apartment in Addison. When they arrived, Debra, Joshua, and Jordan were in the swimming pool.

Gilbert also saw Laverne Ward, who was walking around outside the fence that enclosed the swimming pool. Gilbert had nothing to say to Ward. He still remembered that first time he met Ward in 1993.

While he was visiting Debra and the kids in her Hanover apartment, Ward kicked open the door. He said he wanted to talk to Debra and they went into a back room. Gilbert did not hear what was said.

Going outside, Gilbert saw two male friends waiting for Ward.

When Ward came out, he talked briefly with Gilbert and pointedly told him to stay away from Debra.

Gilbert answered that he could not do that. He said Samantha was his daughter and that he "had nothing going on with Debra."

Ward again told Gilbert to stay away, adding that he didn't want to be held responsible for what he could do to him.

Scott Gilbert and his wife planned to return to Addison in November 1995 for Thanksgiving. Scott's sister and Mrs. Gilbert's family lived in the Addison area.

On Sunday, November 12, 1995, Gilbert phoned to talk to Samantha. Debra answered the phone, and during their talk she asked him if he would take all of the children if something happened to her. He wanted to know why she was so concerned about "something happening to her," because in the past two months when they talked, she had asked that question four or five times. But she did not explain.

Gilbert remembered that Debra had told him some time earlier that she was having problems with Ward. She did not elaborate because she never discussed with Gilbert what was happening in her life.

Only five days after that Sunday conversation with Debra, the shocking news reached Gilbert that Debra, Samantha, and Joshua had been murdered and the baby that she was expecting had been torn from her womb by the killers. The horrible news left Gilbert in a state of shock and grief as he prepared to go to Addison for the funeral services.

Detectives had a list of Evans's friends compiled from interviews with her sister, mother, and James Edwards, and from Evans's phone records.

Cynthia Sawyer was on the list.

"Debbie was my best friend," she told the investigators. They had met in 1989. Sawyer said she was the one who had introduced her to Laverne Ward when Evans was living in Carol Stream. Cynthia herself had met Ward through one of his longtime girlfriends, whom Cynthia also knew.

Evans and Sawyer alternated in baby-sitting with each other's children. During the round-robin of baby-sitting and back-and-forth visiting, Samantha had become one of Cynthia's daughter's best friends.

It was Evans who took Cynthia Sawyer to the hospital for the birth of her son. Sawyer was planning to do the same for Evans, who had intended to enter the hospital on Sunday, November 19, to have the birth of her fourth child induced on the advice of her doctor.

"I was going to baby-sit with her kids while she was in the hospital," Sawyer said, "and pick her up when she got out."

Sawyer said she had talked with Evans on the phone twice on the day of the murders. The first conversation was early in the afternoon, and the last time she ever talked to her was about 5:30 P.M.

"We were talking basically about old times," Cynthia said. "When our children grew up together, Debbie was my baby-sitter. And she was supposed to watch one of my little ones the next day, Friday. We talked about me taking her to the hospital, keeping her kids, and picking her up."

During their talk there were several interruptions, Sawyer recalled.

Debbie had call-waiting. "She would get a call and I would just hold on."

She also could hear Evans's children in the background.

Before they finished talking, Evans had told her—after several interrupting calls—"I wish these people would leave me alone." She did not mention any names.

Shortly after that, Evans said, "Just a minute. Someone's at the door." Sawyer heard the door open and Joshua Evans say, "It's Verne." The boy habitually called Ward "Verne," one of the names he had mentioned as the killers of his mother and sister.

Seconds after hearing Joshua's words as to who was at the door, Sawyer had heard another voice, which she recognized as that of Laverne Ward.

The women had ended their phone conversation at that point.

Sawyer contributed some other vital information during her police interview. She said she also knew Annette Williams, but not as well as she did Evans. She said she had visited in Williams's Schaumburg home "two or three times the week of the murders," before they happened. One of the visits may have been on the actual day of the slayings, she thought.

"It would have been the fifteenth or sixteenth of November," Sawyer said. "Annette had called me. She needed me to take her to the store. She said her car was broke down."

During the visit she had noticed Williams had an Ace bandage on her right arm. In fact, she had observed the light-brown Ace bandage both of the times she visited that week.

Sawyer related that Evans first revealed she was again pregnant during a visit in Sawyer's home.

The women had other conversations about Evans's pregnancy. In one of the last talks together, Evans told Sawyer she had had an ultrasound test that showed the baby was a boy.

She already had decided on a name, Eli, or Elijah, chosen because that was the middle name of her boyfriend, James Edwards, according to Sawyer.

The detectives also learned from Sawyer that during a conversation with Annette Williams in "either 1993 or 1994," Williams had confided that she could not have any more children because her tubes had been tied. But after that—several different times—Annette had told everybody that she was pregnant again and Sawyer had not been sure what to believe.

Detectives later had Sawyer drop by the police station to make a statement about what she had told them, and to look at the Ace bandage found on a bed in the murder apartment.

She identified the bandage as looking like the one that Williams had on her arm.

FOURTEEN

Premeditated murder is like a forest fire. They both can start with a spark that finally rages out of control. Months before the heinous Evans family murders of November 16, 1995, Laverne Ward had exhibited violent feelings for killing Debra Evans.

His hatred and desire to murder the mother of his child Jordan was disclosed in an explosive incident in the apartment of Annette Williams and Fedell Caffey, who were then living on North Avenue in Villa Park.

The incident came to light after the killings when a woman who had witnessed Ward's angry outburst over Evans made a telephone call in December 1995 to the State Attorney's Office in Wheaton.

The caller, who gave the name of a female friend instead of her own—thus hoping to avoid identification and subsequent involvement—reported that Ward had flown into a rage, smashed his fist through a wall of the town house and said he wanted to kill Evans "now."

That had been in May 1995, about six months before it happened. This apparently was when the plot to kill Evans and take her expected baby had begun to form among the three conspirators.

Addison detectives traced the true identity of the caller through the friend's name she had given.

The witness's name was Myra Redding, and when the detectives located her, Redding told her story. She also explained why she had not given her name: She feared reprisal from Fedell Caffey. Redding said that her husband, after she told him about Ward's violent outbreak, warned her of possible harm by someone if she did not keep quiet about what happened.

"If you say anything, you're a dead bitch," Redding quoted her husband as saying.

She told the detectives that she went to the home of Caffey and Williams to borrow a vacuum cleaner and was there when an enraged Ward arrived and smashed his fist through a wall.

"I want to kill her! Let's do it now!" Ward shouted, or words to that effect as remembered by Redding.

He was killing-mad over Evans's restrictions on his visits to Jordan, Redding recalled.

Recounting her story, she said that Fedell Caffey seemed agreeable enough to the proposed homicide, asking Ward, "Do you want me to get a knife or a gun?"

"I don't care," Ward replied.

Annette Williams cautioned Ward to "chill it," to wait for a while or it would be obvious that Ward had done it, Redding recalled.

The hole punched in the wall had been patched after that, but an investigator later noticed what looked like a patch. Although it blended fairly well with the white wall, the patch still was apparent and the investigator had taken measurements and made a diagram of its location.

When a detective questioned the apartment complex manager about the damage from Ward's fist, the manager said he did not remember a hole in the wall—it had been a long time since the damage—but he did say that he had taken the entire security deposit put up by Williams and Caffey before they moved out.

James Edwards, in his ongoing talks with the detectives, remembered another incident that had seemed strange at the time, but now was seen as further evidence that the plans for murdering Evans and taking her baby had been under way for several months before they were carried out.

About one week before the murders, Edwards answered a knock at the apartment door. Standing there was a woman whom he did not know. She asked for Debra, and Edwards said she was not there.

The woman said she and Evans had a luncheon engagement that day. Edwards had not heard Debra mention it, and she always told him if she had some special thing she was going to do. But he only repeated that Debra wasn't home.

The woman kept talking.

What's going on anyway, Edwards wondered. She started asking all kinds of questions: What time did he go to work? How did he get there, walk? What street did he take? What time did he get off?

The puzzled Edwards wondered why this woman he didn't even know was being so nosy about his work schedule. But he replied he went to work about 6:00 P.M. and finished about 2:30 A.M. He was getting tired of this conversation, and he didn't answer her question of which way he went to get there and back.

It went on, as he recalled, for about ten or fifteen minutes.

Finally the funny-acting woman with all the questions about his working hours said to tell Debbie she came by, and she left.

It was not until later when he saw the same woman at the Addison Police Station on November 17 that he learned her name was Annette Williams. And then he realized what the quiz session a week earlier had been all about.

The pestering woman had wanted to know when he wasn't home so they could come then and kill the three people he considered to be his family.

Other evidence came to light that the murder of Debra Evans and the stealing of her yet-to-be-born baby had been planned for some time.

The investigation turned up information that three weeks before November 16, Annette Williams made an application for a free holiday gift basket from Milton Township, specifying she wanted it for her son.

An employee of the Milton Township government office located in Wheaton revealed Williams had requested a Thanksgiving gift basket for her son Fedell.

One week before the triple murders, Williams told DuPage County probation officer Darlene Bearden, who was her probation officer in 1995, that she had just given birth to a baby boy.

Aware of the intensive investigation going on after Williams's arrest, Bearden told the investigators about Williams's statement.

"She said it was a boy," said Bearden, who related that Williams told her on September 28 that "she was pregnant and her baby was due in three weeks."

When Williams saw the probation officer again on November 9, "she said she had just had a baby," Bearden said.

She told the county worker that she and her boyfriend, Fedell Caffey, the father of the baby, planned to marry in December.

Bearden added, "I told her to bring me verification that she had a baby. . . . She didn't."

As the police learned from her sister Tina Martin and her mother, Martha Martin, Williams had been telling them and friends since April 1995 that she was expecting. First she said the baby was due in August; later she changed the date to September, then October, and finally made the 3:30 A.M. call on November 17 to her sister claiming her baby had been born.

After seeing the baby, neither of Williams's relatives had believed it was Annette's baby.

The life of Jacqueline Annette Williams paralleled that of Debra Evans in three ways: She had been raised in a close-knit, religious family. Like Evans, she had three children. And she also found herself romantically involved with live-in boyfriends in the last few years who had frequently abused her.

But unlike Evans, she did become involved in drugs—both as a crack cocaine user and as a girlfriend of an active drug dealer, Fedell Caffey. She had had several minor brushes with the law herself—mostly with offenses such as theft and forgery, but serious enough to end up on probation.

Annette Williams and her family were natives of Alabama. After giving birth to Annette in 1966, her mother was divorced and moved with her three children to Chicago, hoping to find a better life.

But Chicago's south side where they lived was a tough, crime-ridden area, teeming with drug traffic and gang violence.

Seeking better schools for the children, Martha Martin moved again, this time taking her children to live near relatives in the Chicago western suburban town of Wheaton.

Wheaton, the county seat of DuPage County, was a quiet town with a Bible college. Dr. Billy Graham once had been a student at the college, and Red Grange, the legendary football great, was from Wheaton.

Growing up in the peaceful small town, Annette was a student at Lowell Elementary School, Franklin Middle School, and Wheaton Central High School, where she was a flag girl. She was well liked and had many friends.

Williams's childhood had been a normal one. She was a good student and regularly attended a Baptist church on Sunday and sang in the church choir.

One of her relatives once described Williams as "a

daddy's girl," who got along with her mother and "very well with her father."

At the age of sixteen and in her sophomore year of high school, Williams started changing. She quit getting home on time. She quit going to church regularly. She became pregnant and dropped out of school.

At the age of seventeen, Annette got married. The couple lived in Carol Stream and had three children. All of her children were delivered by cesarean section. Williams and her husband were divorced in 1990.

In 1993, Williams attended a vocational school and was certified as a nurse's aide.

One summer day in 1994, as Fedell Caffey was driving down a street in Haywood, he noticed a striking young woman walking along the same street. He struck up a conversation with the woman, Annette Williams.

That was the beginning of their live-in relationship. Friends of the couple said they fought frequently, usually about Caffey occasionally leaving to visit another girlfriend who was the mother of his young daughter.

One of Caffey's friends speculated that Caffey may have been drawn to Williams because she was several years older than he was, a woman "he might have thought he could have a family with."

At the time Caffey was twenty-two and Williams twenty-eight.

The friend said that Annette once stabbed Caffey "for going out with friends." Caffey had not reported the stabbing to police.

"Annette was friendly . . . but she was possessive, and when it came to Fedell, she was crazy, psychotic. She'd do anything," said the friend.

Neighbors of the couple had a different viewpoint. To them, Caffey was violent and scary; Williams seemed friendly and quiet.

Tina Martin believed that one of her sister's failings in life was being too trusting of people, especially the men in her life. Williams frequently had been beaten by her live-in boyfriends. But they always got back together again.

In trying to figure out what happened along the way to a normal and happy girl, her mother once tearfully told a reporter, "There are a lot of pieces to the puzzle missing. She loved people too much. Not just kids, but all people. She's not the monster everyone thinks she is. She can be influenced by a lot of people. She likes to do what other people do."

Williams took good care of her own children and others with whom she was a baby-sitter, her friends said. In fact, Williams was so good with children that the small son of Tina Martin called her "his second mom," the sister said.

Tina Martin also described Williams as easily led by other people. "She's too trusting of people. She befriends anyone."

A psychologist who examined Williams reported she was easily influenced, had a dependent personality, and especially was vulnerable to predatory men. She endured abuse by such male friends. If she left, she always returned, or let the boyfriend return.

"Threats from such males would cause her to do things she would not initiate," the psychologist said.

Williams's sister recalled that once in 1984 she was summoned to a police station after Fedell Caffey had throttled Williams.

Remembering Williams's bruised and swollen face, the sister said, "If I wouldn't have known she was my sister, I wouldn't have recognized her."

Now, under arrest for the murder of Debra Evans and her two children and the kidnapping of baby Elijah from the womb, Williams had stated her motive simply in the signed confession she gave:

"For our entire relationship together, my boyfriend Fedell had been trying to get me pregnant so that he could have a baby boy. For the longest time he has told me he has 2 requirements for our child together—that we have a boy and that it is light-skinned so that it resembles him."

Annette knew that she could not oblige her boyfriend. Her tubes had been tied. But she was desperate to please him.

And she knew where she could get the exact kind of baby Fedell demanded.

To the homicide detectives, her desperation to comply with Fedell's wishes was the whole motive behind the slaughters on November 16, 1995, on North Swift Road in Addison.

FIFTEEN

The investigation swung back to Laverne Ward, twenty-four, who, after being located by Detectives Van Stedum and Simo, had denied any involvement in the murders of Debra and Samantha Evans and the taking of Debra's full-term baby.

Ward was born and grew up in Fairhope, Alabama. After dropping out of high school, he moved to the Chicago area. He started getting into trouble in 1990 when he was arrested on suspicion of underage drinking.

Since then, he had been jailed on various charges, which included beating up girlfriends, fighting with the cops who arrested him, and dealing drugs.

The investigators again turned their attention to Ward. He told the detectives that he had spent Thursday, the day of the crimes, visiting friends and relatives and had not even seen Annette Williams or Fedell Caffey that day.

Checking out Ward's alibi had been interrupted by the discovery of Joshua Evans's body in Maywood. Now, backtracking on Ward's whereabouts, the detectives questioned one of the suspect's relatives, forty-eight-year-old John Pettaway of Wheaton.

Pettaway was known by his pals and family members as "T.T."

"I was real little and my grandma called me that 'cause of the two 'T's' in my name," Pettaway said with a grin. He had known Annette all her life and Annette's cousin Ward since he was about three years old, he told the detectives.

Pettaway said he was with Ward for several hours on the Thursday of the murders, visiting some friends and relatives before he had to go to work later that night, working the third shift from 11:00 P.M. to 7:00 A.M.

After he got up on Thursday, Pettaway had first washed his car and later—about 2:30 P.M.—driven over to see Ward, who, he knew, was staying with a girlfriend named Laura. She lived in an apartment on Roosevelt Road.

Ward had accompanied Pettaway from his girlfriend's apartment. When they drove away, Ward spotted Annette Williams and Fedell Caffey in their gray four-door Mercury Sable. He asked Pettaway to turn around and stop so he could talk to them.

Ward got out and went over to the gray car. Pettaway did not hear any of the conversation, but the three had talked for ten to fifteen minutes, he recalled.

Pettaway and Ward then went to the home of Pettaway's brother in Wheaton. As they got out of the car to go inside, Pettaway noticed Williams and Caffey driving down the street toward them.

The couple pulled over and stopped, and Ward walked to the car to talk to them again. When they left, Ward came in and drank some beer with Pettaway and his brother.

Leaving there, Ward wanted Pettaway to drive him to a store in Carol Stream where his girlfriend worked so he could get some money from her. Next they stopped to visit another friend.

It was party time. Several people were there, drinking beer and smoking "Mo Premo," a mixture of crack cocaine and tobacco in a cigarette, Pettaway related. Ward and Pettaway stayed for several hours.

Ward asked Pettaway on early Thursday evening to drop him by a local school to see if he could find Caffey. A basketball game was being played at the school. Annette Williams's son was one of the players, and Ward figured Caffey might be there. But he didn't find him.

They drove to Carol Stream to pick up Pettaway's girlfriend. Pettaway later took Ward to another relative's house on Crescent Street.

Then he took his girlfriend to her place and returned to his own apartment to grab a few hours' sleep before going to work at 11:00 P.M.

Pettaway remembered that he ran into Annette Williams the next day about 2:00 P.M. at a car wash. She had her kids with her, and they were busy vacuuming the backseat area of the same four-door gray car he had seen them in Thursday afternoon, he said.

Pettaway said he had a brief conversation with Williams.

"She asked me if I knew Verne was in jail, and I asked her what he was in jail for. She said it was for murder and that he wanted her to come up there.

"I asked her why don't you go up there then, and she said she didn't want to have nothing to do with it.

She said Verne wanted her to tell them that he was with her the whole time."

"Did you know Debra Evans?" a detective asked.

"Yeah, I knew her. I had met her once in Hanover, when Verne was living with her."

The last time he had seen Evans was in August or September when she and "everyone was at a barbecue out on Roosevelt Road—Verne, Annette, Fedell, and a bunch of other people."

Pettaway had punched holes in Ward's version of his activities that Thursday. Ward not only had seen Annette and Verne that afternoon—he had talked to them at least twice for fifteen minutes or so each time. And he had looked for Caffey after that at the ball game.

When talking casually to Detective Bill Cooley when he first was picked up, Ward mentioned that he had been out of town Thursday night, in Chicago, visiting a friend.

Following up on this bit of information, detectives with the help of Cook County investigators learned that Ward had a friend who lived on Douglas Park, in a part of town known as an "open air" drug market.

When detectives talked to this friend, he recalled that Ward had a Walkman-type portable radio or stereo with him when he came to the friend's house in Chicago. It had two speakers on the side. The friend thought Ward was trying to sell it to buy drugs in that area.

At the time the detectives did not give any special significance to Ward's trying to sell a portable stereo. They were unaware then that such a boom box had belonged to little Samantha Evans and had been taken from the murder scene.

Ward's claims of innocence were falling apart

Ward's alibi continued to crumble when the detectives went to the residence of another of his relatives—an uncle who lived in Wheaton—who, the murder suspect said, could verify his whereabouts during the crucial time period when the killings were believed to have happened.

The detectives also talked separately to two fifteen-year-old girls who were present at the house. They both recalled that Ward had come by the apartment that night.

However, it was not until much later in the investigation that one of the girls reported that Ward had come in carrying a plastic grocery bag with what looked like clothing inside and had gone directly to the bathroom and changed clothes.

At this later interview the teenager mentioned for the first time that Ward's clothing was bloody when he arrived: "His clothes were messed up. He had blood on the top of his shirt and on his pants."

She said she earlier had withheld the information about the blood because her uncle had urged her not to say anything to the police. He at one time had been suspected by police as being the fourth of the "four burglars" seen by Joshua Evans.

She said Ward went outside and "got into a gray car where a woman with big 'Afro-like hair' and a man were waiting."

The other girl had not noticed any blood on Ward at that time. But she said she had seen Ward come into the apartment and that he had changed his clothes while there.

She said she had been really busy—doing homework, baby-sitting four smaller children, and watching TV. She had noticed little more than Ward's coming and going after he changed clothes.

But the girl did recall that the next morning when they rode the school bus together, the other girl had told her she had noticed blood on Ward's clothing.

She remembered, too, that after sitting in the car outside for a few minutes, Ward came back into the apartment and had a conversation with her mother, who had just arrived.

The girl told the investigators she heard her mother tell Ward to invite Debbie Evans for Thanksgiving dinner at their home. Ward had said "he wasn't going to be talking to Debbie anymore," the girl said.

The girl who finally admitted she had seen blood on Ward's clothes also recalled that a family pet, a pit bull, was "going nuts." When she went outside to see what was wrong, she saw three people in a gray car whom she didn't know. Later, after seeing the suspects' pictures on television, she identified two of the people as Annette Williams and Fedell Caffey. She still did not recognize the other person.

The investigators wondered if the dog had been set off by the smell of blood on Ward's clothing.

On January 11, 1996, Detective Van Stedum was making one last walk-through in the North Swift Road apartment. Once the comfortable home for a small family, it had been locked and guarded all this time since that horrible early Friday morning when the homicide probe began.

Van Stedum was accompanied by James Edwards, who, it was believed, would be more aware than anyone else of anything unusual or missing.

It was a painful experience for the grieving Edwards, the only adult survivor of so many happy days here.

Now it was a place of stale air and haunting silence, smeared with fingerprint powder and with large parts cut from the carpeting for bloodstain analysis. Even some furniture had been taken for testing, such as the small love seat beside which Debra Evans's gutted body had been found by Edwards.

The sickening presence of the bloody violence in the quiet apartment was almost tangible.

After this last inspection by the investigators, the apartment would be freed from all the security—the police padlocks and the sealing tape and the around-the-clock police guard. Relatives would then be allowed to come and remove the personal items of their slain loved ones.

Van Stedum was standing near the hutch adjacent to the sliding glass door that opened onto a small patio area.

What suddenly caught the detective's eye was a piece of paper that appeared to be bloodstained. When Van Stedum donned gloves and examined the paper closely, he saw that it was a legal notice, a vehicle emission notice that is mailed out by the state when it is time for a vehicle emission inspection.

Near the bottom edge of the paper was what appeared to be faint fingerprint ridges within the bloodstain on the document. Somehow the stained paper had been overlooked in the first search for clues in the apartment, not surprising considering the voluminous amount of evidence that had been gathered for analysis.

The detective had an evidence technician collect the notice for later examination in the crime lab. The emission notice would turn out to be one of the strongest pieces of evidence found in the apartment.

The partial fingerprint later was identified definitely as that of Annette Williams. It was almost as if she had left her name written in blood.

SIXTEEN

The DuPage County Judicial Office Facility is a stately four-story building located in the group of county buildings on North County Farm Road. Its structural beauty belies the sometimes unpleasant legal events that unfold in the inside courtrooms. The building stands beside a serene lake that is populated with flocks of transit ducks and other waterfowl. There are outside picnic tables where visitors and court employees and other county personnel can enjoy peaceful, picniclike lunches.

In front of the building is an enclosed bus booth with benches for the people who ride the public transportation to and from the court building or other nearby county offices.

Large paved parking lots surround the building. Around eight or nine o'clock in the morning, the traffic is heavy, with employees parking and walking to their offices. The same scene repeats itself at closing time, usually around 5:00 P.M.

The DuPage County Sheriff's Department operates from a three-story building near the court building. An enclosed corridor runs between the sheriff's building to the multistoried county jail, and another tunnel connects the jail and the court facility.

First-floor entrances to the building are guarded by manned electronic security stations. Deputies are on duty during all hours that the building is open to the public.

Security is as tight as that of any large airport. There are conveyors on which to place briefcases, billfolds, purses, or anything else that attorneys, witnesses, or the general public might carry into the building. The upper floors are accessible by escalator or elevators.

An excellent cafeteria operates on the ground floor for the convenience of employees and the public.

The DuPage County State Attorney's Office occupies a large suite on the third floor. Once again, any visitor must pass through the reception areas before being admitted through electronically controlled doors to the attorneys' offices.

The State Attorney's Office is a maze of small partitioned cubicles for the large staff of assistant attorneys and secretarial employees. The higher-ups have glassed-in offices along the sides and at the ends of the cubicle area. There are conference rooms where lawyers and witnesses can talk.

An unfamiliar visitor can wander aimlessly through the partitioned cubicles until rescued by a helpful secretary. The crowded layout is evocative of those puzzle maps that used to appear on the Sunday comic pages, with a center starting point to work from with a pencil through the intricate network of lines to reach the outside.

Beginning on early Friday, November 17, 1995, when ASA Tom Epach was called out to work alongside the homicide detectives and evidence technicians, the State Attorney's Office became the focal point of an intensive, around-the-clock investigation that would go on for weeks.

Old-timers could remember only a few such shocking crimes in the past that had so electrified the whole state of Illinois. The triple murders of a pregnant mother and her two children and the unimaginable abduction of a full-term infant torn from the mother's womb later was described by a prosecutor as "like something out of a Stephen King novel."

Three assistant state attorneys were named by DuPage County state attorney Anthony "Tony" Peccareili to head up the preparation of the case for later trial: Tom Epach, a veteran former Cook County prosecutor, and assistant state attorneys John Kinsella and Michael Wolfe.

When Epach decided to return to work for the Cook County State Attorney's Office in 1996, assistant state attorney Jeffrey C. Kendall replaced him on the Evans case prosecution team.

Meanwhile, Peccareili himself changed jobs, going to the State Attorney General's Office, and DuPage

County got a newly elected state attorney in the person of Joseph E. Birkett.

John Kinsella is a cheerful, legally astute Irishman who had started in the DuPage County State Attorney's Office in the fall of 1980, working as a clerk and rookie prosecutor in the traffic court while still in law school. He went to work full-time as soon as he obtained his law license in October 1981, after graduating from Northern Illinois University in DeKalb.

In 1995, Kinsella, barely forty years old and a family man with five children, had risen through the ranks to the post of deputy chief of criminal prosecution and had moved up to first assistant state attorney by the time Annette Williams went to trial in 1996.

Kinsella always had been interested in history and political science, and eventually his decision to go to law school was a spin-off from those college subjects.

His Irish parents had immigrated directly to Chicago in 1953 from Scotland, where they then were living. Before that, they had resided in southern Ireland.

Two years after their arrival in Chicago, John Kinsella was born in the big city. He grew up and attended schools there.

Jeff Kendall was another native Illinoisan. Born in the little town of Watseka, about seventy miles south of Wheaton on the Indiana-Illinois state line, he graduated from high school there, then attended DePauw University in Green Castle, Indiana. Two years later he transferred to Illinois State University, from where he graduated.

After college he went to Marquette University Law School and came to the DuPage County State Attorney's Office right after law school.

The thirty-nine-year-old Kendall is not married. He figures it is easier with the job he has to be a bachelor, because the hours get crazy sometimes.

Kendall was bitten with the law bug while still in college.

"I took some classes that got me involved in some criminal law and constitutional law classes and actually worked part-time for a guy who was a defense attorney. I would go over to the jail and interview his clients. I got real interested in criminal law."

He also worked for a couple of judges and soon decided to take the law school entrance exam.

Upon getting his law degree, Kendall interned for a while in the Cook County State Attorney's Office, and after taking the bar exam, he came to the DuPage County State Attorney's Office.

"I wanted to do trial work, I enjoyed being in a courtroom. They asked me to start here, and I took the job the next day and have been here ever since."

By 1999 he was deputy chief of the criminal division.

Michael Wolfe was born in Oak Park, Illinois, Ernest Hemingway's hometown. Throughout his education he attended Catholic schools. He obtained his law degree from John Marshall Law School in Chicago, which he attended from 1981 through 1984.

Wolfe became interested in criminal law as a youth because of the Richard Speck murder case. He knew and visited with a lawyer, who lived down the block, whose name was William J. Martin. Martin became one of the state's most famous attorneys after he prosecuted Richard Speck. He later cowrote a book with Chicago writer Dennis Breo on the Speck case titled *Crime of the Century*.

Wolfe was helping Martin move some of his files into his law office one day.

"I accidentally came across the Richard Speck file. I remember seeing a photo of Speck, some crime scene pictures, an enlarged fingerprint. I later read the Speck murder trial transcripts. That's how I got interested in law, and from the very start, as a result of seeing the Speck file, I wanted to be a prosecutor."

For a while he worked as a law clerk for Martin. There was a generation gap between the two men, but Wolfe and Martin had attended the same high school.

Wolfe still plays in an amateur hockey league every Sunday with his good friend, Martin. In fact, the forty-year-old Wolfe is an accomplished athlete who regularly participates in triathlons, the endurance races that combine swimming, bicycling, and running.

He once rode his Harley-Davidson motorcycle across the country and is an enthusiastic rugby player. He was now facing a different sort of major endurance test, the investigation and legal preparation for the trials of the three suspects being held without bond in the county jail.

Victims Debra Evans, 28, Samantha, 10, and Joshua, 7.
Jordon, 17 months, was unharmed.
(Photo courtesy Illinois State Attorney's Office)

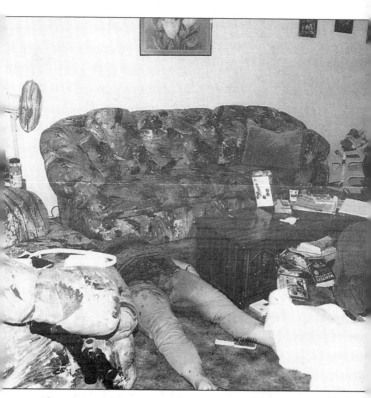

The nine-month pregnant Evans's slacks were pulled back up after killers brutally removed her baby from her body.
(Photo courtesy Illinois State Attorney's Office)

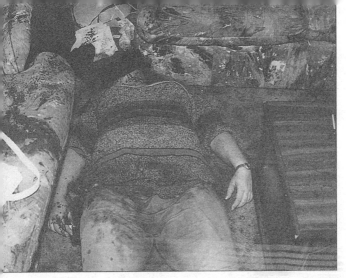

Evans had been shot in the head, stabbed several times, and had a gaping thirteen-inch wound across her lower abdomen. (*Photo courtesy Illinois State Attorney's Office*)

Blood from Evans's wounds spurted onto the furniture and pooled on the carpet. (*Photo courtesy Illinois State Attorney's Office*)

The bathroom vanity sink, the walls behind the vanity
and the floor were all blood-spattered.
(*Photo courtesy Illinois State Attorney's Office*)

Police found the bloody poultry shears with a broken handle used to cut Debra open and stab Samantha on the sidewalk in front of Evans's apartment.
(*Photo courtesy Illinois State Attorney's Office*)

F.B.I. divers found the .25 caliber gun used
to shoot Debra Evans in Lake Herrick.
(*Photo courtesy Illinois State Attorney's Office*)

The wooden-handled butcher knife used in the murders
was found in Williams's dishwasher.
(*Photo courtesy Illinois State Attorney's Office*)

Blood and cuts on Samantha Evans's right hand were defensive wounds, showing she'd tried to fight off her killers. (*Photo courtesy Illinois State Attorney's Office*)

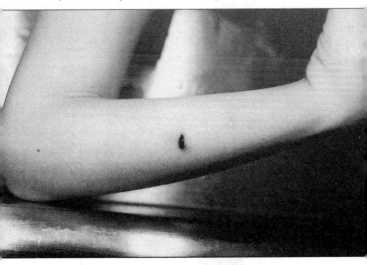

Defensive cut on Samantha Evans's arm. (*Photo courtesy Illinois State Attorney's Office*)

Joshua Evans was found in an alley with his coat over his head. (*Photo courtesy Illinois State Attorney's Office*)

Joshua Evans had been stabbed and strangled.
(*Photo courtesy Illinois State Attorney's Office*)

Police found the white electrical cord used to strangle
Joshua Evans in the garage of the killers' townhouse.
(*Photo courtesy Illinois State Attorney's Office*)

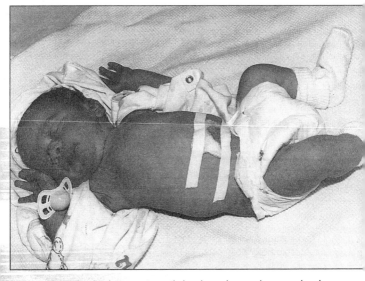

Although Elijah Evans's umbilical cord was damaged, when examined at the hospital, he was found to be in excellent condition. (*Photo courtesy Illinois State Attorney's Office*)

Jacqueline Annette Williams, 28, was charged with first-degree murder, aggravated kidnapping, and armed robbery.
(*Photo courtesy Illinois State Attorney's Office*)

Fedell Caffey, 22, Williams's boyfriend, was also
charged with murder, kidnapping and robbery.
(*Photo courtesy Illinois State Attorney's Office*)

Laverne Ward, 24, Williams's cousin, and the father of both
Elijah and Jordon, was the third person charged.
(*Photo courtesy Illinois State Attorney's Office*)

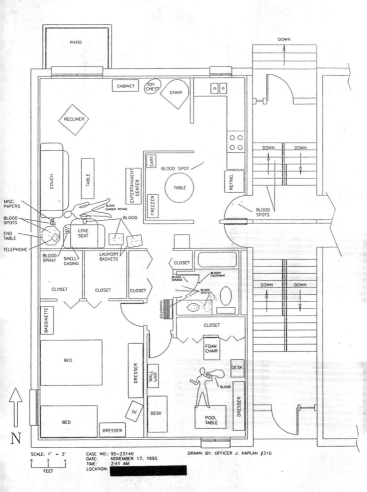

Police crime scene diagram of Evans's apartment showing locations of bodies, blood spots, and bloody footprint.
(*Photo courtesy Illinois State Attorney's Office*)

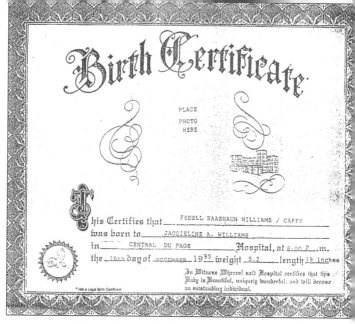

Birth Certificate

PLACE
PHOTO
HERE

This Certifies that ___FEDELL RAASHAUN WILLIAMS / CAFFY___
was born to ___JACQIELINE A. WILLIAMS___
in ___CENTRAL DU PAGE___ Hospital, at 8:00 P.m.
the ___16th day of NOVEMBER 19 95___ weight ___5.3___ length ___19 inches___

In Witness Whereof said Hospital certifies that this Baby is Beautiful, uniquely wonderful, and will become an outstanding individual.

* Not a Legal Birth Certificate

Williams had a phony birth certificate made to
back up her claim of having given birth to a son.
(*Photo courtesy Illinois State Attorney's Office*)

NEWBORN PHYSICAL DISCHARGE INFORMATION

Name ___FEDELL R. WILLIAMS CAFFY___ Date of Birth ___11-16-95___ Discharge Date ___11-16-95___

Birth Weight ___5.6___ Discharge Weight ___5.3___ Apgars _____

Length ___19 INCHES___ Head Circumference ___34.5___ Hct. (if done) _____

Cord Blood results, Type, Rh, & Coombs (if done) ___A POS.___

Significant History & Findings ___HEALTHY NEWBORN MALE___

___FOLLOW UP WITH WHEATON MEDICAL CLINIC___

Police found a phony physical discharge information
sheet for the baby at Williams's home.
(*Photo courtesy Illinois State Attorney's Office*)

Addison, Illinois police detectives (*left to right*)
Mark van Stedum, Paul Hardt, Dave Wall,
Cathy Vrchota, Mike Simo, and Joe Lullo.
(*Photo courtesy Addison, Illinois, Police Department*)

(*Left to right*) First Assistant State's Attorney John Kinsella,
Deputy Chief of the Criminal Prosecutions Bureau
Jeff Kendall, Assistant State's Attorney Elizabeth Ekl, and
Chief of the Criminal Prosecutions Bureau Michael Wolfe,
receiving national award for their roles in this case from
DuPage County, Illinois State's Attorney Joseph Birkett.
(*Photo courtesy Illinois State Attorney's Office*)

In 1985, Wolfe began working in the DuPage County State Attorney's Office as an assistant state attorney in the traffic court section.

Working his way up over the years, Wolfe became chief of the criminal bureau over all criminal prosecutions from traffic court up, with sixty-two attorneys under his supervision.

Sometimes he marvels at the irony that it was killer Richard Speck who ignited an interest and determination in Wolfe that set him on the way to becoming a state prosecutor of other brutal killers, like the three people charged with the Evans family murders.

SEVENTEEN

The legal battles in any case—especially a major murder case—begin long before the opposing attorneys square off in a courtroom before a jury.

The preparation that goes into a high-profile case is the roll-up-the-sleeves groundwork by both sides that they hope will mean a victory when it all goes before the jury.

Before anything else, the state attorneys had to present their evidence to a county grand jury to obtain indictments against the accused trio.

Meanwhile, the defense lawyers—attorneys from the Public Defenders Office for Annette Williams and Fedell Caffey, who did not have the money to hire lawyers, and a notable Chicago defense attorney for Laverne Ward (after his first lawyer withdrew)—began the legal dueling that would continue through the next two years before the actual jury trials started.

Not unexpectedly, the defense attorneys during the next months attacked several issues, including the legality of the arrest of the three defendants, and the admissibility of Williams's signed confession. There would be other issues raised by the state and the defense.

Undoubtedly, one of the most important ones to both

sides was whether the jury would be allowed to hear the last words spoken by Joshua Evans as remembered by the state's key witnesses, Patrice Scott and Dwight Pruitt. With those words, Joshua had named the killers.

Because of events in the lives of the two witnesses, the defense was expected to target their credibility and thus the admissibility of their testimony.

The prosecution, in a sense, would be bringing the little victim's words from the grave if his damning statements overheard by Scott and Pruitt were allowed by the trial judge.

The judicial rulings on these points would bear heavily on the verdicts the juries would return.

Evidence and witnesses in the three separate murder trials would be different, and the state attorneys had to sort out which witnesses would be called in each of the trials. The prosecutors anticipated that the defense, which would be put forward for the defendants, would be, in a nutshell, ABM—Anybody But Me.

Long hours of preparation and more preparation. That would determine the outcome.

As prosecutor Mike Wolfe recalled, "During the preparation period, prosecutors had to sacrifice their personal lives and work long overtime hours. We knew it would take every ounce of effort and energy in order to be effective in the Evans prosecution."

The same was true, of course, for the defense lawyers, who realized they had an uphill battle facing them in DuPage County's most notorious homicide case in many years.

* * *

A DuPage County grand jury began hearing evidence in the macabre murders on November 22, not quite a week after the slayings occurred. Police investigators and other witnesses paraded before the investigative body over the next two weeks.

Meanwhile, acting on information gained from Williams, the Addison police again talked to Betty Larson, the friend of Williams's to whose house the newborn infant boy had been taken after he was removed from Evans's womb.

Larson identified herself as a businesswoman who operated a housecleaning and maid service. She was told by detectives that she had been linked to the murder investigation as the person who reportedly supplied the gun that killed Evans. The distraught woman at first denied the accusation, but finally she broke down and led the investigators to where she said the gun had been discarded by her and a friend named Alice Pirtle.

The pond was within the Herrick Lake Forest Preserve, close to Herrick and Butterfield Roads, outside of Wheaton.

A diving team supplied by the FBI started searching in the water on Saturday, December 2, 1995, and it wasn't long before an FBI diver surfaced holding a small silver gun in his hand. The gun was a .25-caliber automatic that almost fit in the palm of the hand.

Police photographers snapped photos of the diver holding the gun and close-ups of the small weapon.

As a result of questioning Larson, the detectives also arrested two other people said to have been involved in obtaining the gun or later disposing of it. They were

Alice Pirtle, thirty-six, of Wheaton and Maurice Wuertz, twenty-four, of Berwyn.

Larson revealed that she had obtained the weapon from her cousin Wuertz at the request of Annette Williams, who said a gun was needed for protection in a drug deal. Within the week before the murders, Larson also had bought ammunition for the gun at a large gun store in Glendale Heights, Illinois.

Larson said when she obtained the gun and gave it to Williams she had no idea it would be used in a murder.

The detectives also learned that the automatic had jammed after the first shot fired into Debra Evans. Later, when the gun was returned to Larson, she gave it to Wuertz, who had repaired it. But on November 26, 1995, ten days after the murders, the gun was tossed into the pond after Pirtle had used vinegar and a cloth diaper to wipe off fingerprints, detectives were told.

Ballistic tests showed the gun had fired the .25-caliber bullet recovered from Debra Evans's head. Marks on the shell casing recovered in the Addison apartment and the shell of another slug test-fired from the silver automatic were identical, ballistic experts in the county crime lab reported.

Prosecutors now possessed all of the weapons used to kill the Evans family—the bloody poultry shears found outside the murder apartment, the butcher knife retrieved from the dishwasher tray in the Schaumburg town house of Williams and Caffey, and now the gun.

The suspects involved in the gun transaction were charged with concealing a weapon and obstruction of justice and released on bond the following day. They later were indicted on the charges by a grand jury.

On December 12 the grand jury returned indictments against Williams, Caffey, and Ward charging all three with first-degree murder, aggravated kidnapping, and armed robbery in the Evans slayings, and the abductions of the tiny baby Elijah and Joshua Evans. The robbery charge was based on the alleged theft of Edwards's jacket and Samantha's portable stereo.

The three remained in jail with bond denied.

Williams, Caffey, and Ward entered pleas of not guilty in December 1995, in DuPage County Circuit Court. Prosecutor Kinsella announced that his office would seek the death penalty for the accused killers.

A pretrial hearing in the fall of 1996 to determine if Joshua Evans's statements to Pruitt and Scott before the boy was slain would be admitted in the murder trials again drew the attention of the national news media.

During the hearing before Circuit Court judge Peter Dockery, ASA Epach praised the courage of the little boy who named the killers of his mother and sister and continued to do so even in the face of fear and Williams's threatening command to "shut your mouth!"— an act that sealed his own doom.

Epach argued that the boy's emotional and spontaneous statements to Pruitt and Scott the night before and the morning of his brutal murder—even in the presence of the "burglars" he had persistently named as the killers—fit the facts of the case as revealed by the crime scene and the finding of Joshua's newborn baby brother in the hands of Williams and Caffey.

"He sacrificed his own life to get his mommy's . . . and his sister's killer," said Epach, "or at least to get his final words heard in the courtroom."

He also argued that whatever the character of the two witnesses, Scott and Pruitt, other evidence substantiated their testimony.

The defense lawyers, as expected, hit hard at the couple's credibility, mentioning Pruitt's criminal record and Scott's actions of willingly accompanying Williams to the Schaumburg town house even after hearing Joshua's terrifying story.

On November 7, 1996, Judge Dockery ruled that Joshua's words before his own death were reliable enough to be used in the murder trials. Commenting that even though testimony by people who have died often is excluded because attorneys are unable to make a cross-examination, the judge ruled the boy's words admissible at trial.

"I find that the comment is so particularly trustworthy that cross-examination of Joshua Evans would be of marginal utility," said Judge Dockery. "He was volunteering information, stating what he observed, and repeating the statement in the face of adults' assertion that he was wrong."

The defense attorneys tried to take the ruling in stride.

"It is an important ruling, but it doesn't change our defense at all," said the attorney for Ward, who within a short time would resign from the job on grounds he had been threatened and also had not been paid. "The question of Dwight Pruitt's and Patrice Scott's credibility is still going to be a key issue at trial."

The attorney representing Caffey also commented on the judge's decision. "If the jury believes Patrice Scott, Caffey will be convicted. If the jury doesn't believe Patrice Scott, he will be acquitted."

Another pretrial hearing arose when the defense attorneys learned the State Attorney's Office planned to submit three short hairs removed from the knit cap found lying on Samantha Evans's knee to the FBI for testing by a new DNA procedure.

A new forensic test that had been used only twice before in criminal trials was opposed by the defense. The procedure, known as mitochondria DNA testing, makes it possible to use human elements once thought to be unimportant to make more precise genetic DNA matches with suspects.

Explaining the new technology, an expert said most DNA tests use genetic material from cell nuclei. The new test employs DNA from the mitochondria—tiny cell structures that nourish enzyme activity. The big advantage, the scientists say, is that mitochondrial DNA is hardier. It can be found in hair, bones, or teeth, as long as they are intact.

Also, the technicians are able to get a genetic match with a much smaller sample than that required for standard DNA testing. In this case, the amount of hair was too small for the usual DNA testing.

On the negative side, the new test would destroy the hairs, which would not permit other testing on the evidence.

The judge did allow the new testing method on the hair, but it proved to be a moot decision. No DNA of the suspects was found in the samples. It later was learned that the knit cap belonged to a small neighbor boy for whom Debra Evans had been a baby-sitter, and the knit cap had been left behind accidentally.

Standard DNA tests already had been made on blood samples taken from the three suspects for comparison with the bloodstains found in the death apartment.

Now came the lawyers for Fedell Caffey claiming that their client's arrest had not been legal when he was taken into custody the night of November 17 at the Schaumburg town house.

At a pretrial hearing on May 5, 1997, Caffey's attorneys said that the officers had a warrant of arrest *only* for Annette Williams when the couple was arrested upon returning to their town house.

The defense lawyers admitted that the investigators had information that Williams had a boyfriend named Fedell Caffey and that Caffey also had been in the town house earlier that day when Joshua Evans was taken there before he was murdered.

"The police had a right to question him, but we don't think they had a right to arrest him," one defense attorney told the judge.

Caffey had said he was at home in the town house when Williams and another woman arrived and surprised him with the newborn baby they had with them. According to Caffey, Williams had told him that she and Caffey were the parents of the child.

Caffey also claimed he had been given the blood-stained Grambling jacket by Williams—hours before his arrest the night of November 17.

Kinsella argued that the police had a right to arrest Caffey because he had returned with Williams and the newborn baby. At that time the police had evidence that the baby had been removed from Evans by her killers.

Lieutenant Harold Jenkins testified that earlier on November 17 the investigators had been given information that Caffey and Williams had the baby in their possession. Jenkins said that information was a solid reason for arresting Caffey.

The court upheld the arrest of Caffey. Had Caffey's arrest not been ruled legal, the prosecution would have lost one vital piece of evidence, the bloody jacket worn that night by Caffey.

EIGHTEEN

The pictures, in retrospect, are heartbreaking.

There is the one the detective removed from the living room wall of the apartment to circulate to the news media when the hunt for missing Joshua was started. It is of pretty Debra Evans and her three children: daughter Samantha with a hand on her mom's shoulder; baby Jordan in a red romper, not crying but with a slightly quizzical look on his small face as he sits in his mother's arms; and Joshua, showing a mischievous boylike half grin, standing close beside Jordan.

Everybody who knew Joshua—his family, friends, and playmates—remember him as a courageous and caring kid who always was there to take up for his sister "Sam" and his baby brother. In their conversations Joshua shortened his sister's name to "Sam," as did other relatives and her friends. The name just seemed to fit the happy little girl who liked to draw and dance and take part in various sports, and she was kind of a "second-in-command" overseer of her two brothers.

It was a family group that appeared happy, and their photograph would become widely circulated on the front pages of newspapers and on television screens after the horrors that happened in the Addison apartment, in the backseat of a gray car, and finally ending in a shadowy alleyway in Maywood.

There is another picture of baby Jordan being held by James Edwards, his surrogate father who found him that nightmarish early morning of November 17—a sobbing, terrified little boy who met Edwards at the kitchen door, covered with blood on his feet, hands, and the red sleeper he wore and who finally cried himself to sleep.

He looks so at peace in the photograph of Edwards holding him. He is sound asleep, with his arms folded across his chest.

Then there is the color picture of Samantha, Jordan, and Joshua, the three caught by the camera smiling happily with sister Sam beaming as she holds Jordan with her right hand and Joshua with her left. Joshua, his face pressed against the side of Jordan's head, cheek to cheek, his arms encircling his brother.

Baby Jordan was now the only survivor of that joyful trio in the picture.

There is also the other picture of Jordan held on the lap of his father, Laverne Ward. Ward is wearing a red cap and an orange and black striped shirt. His right arm encircles the boy while he holds the baby's left arm in his own left hand. For the often angry and belligerent Ward, he has a complacent look on his face. The photo was taken not many weeks before the killings.

For hours on that hideous November night when his whole world turned into something better suited for a horror movie, Jordan—only seventeen months old and just beginning to talk—was alone in the apartment where he had seen and heard the sounds of the murders of his mother and sister. He had wallowed in their blood as he went aimlessly from room to room, hopelessly alone and weeping, maybe putting his little hands on his mommy and sister, his feet sticky from the mess on the floor.

As it would become known later after Annette Williams's confession, baby Jordan was on the coffee table in the living room barely inches from where his mother fell after a loud noise; on the table when she was ripped open and the baby within was pulled out.

He had heard infant Elijah's first screams and cries when he was born by the act of murder, ruthlessly pulled from inside his dying mother and drawing his first desperate breaths seconds after his mother gasped her last.

The crime scene photographs of the victims were such a horrible contrast to those earlier family photos that reflected love and happiness.

Described as nothing less than a miracle by the doctors and nurses who attended him in the hospital, Elijah not only survived but thrived as a healthy and normal baby. Later, Elijah and Jordan were taken into the home of their mother's sister Wendy, who kept them for a while.

The images of murder were so fresh in Jordan's mind that he lived in fear. He was so afraid that he would run away from visitors he did not know, curl up in a ball and shake and cry uncontrollably. Or screaming in his sleep, he would sit up with his eyes wide open and staring.

Social workers said Debra's sister had four children of her own, and the addition of the two Evans children made it too difficult for her to handle.

In August 1996, the Illinois Department of Children and Family Services recommended that Sam Evans, the father of Debra—who was willing to take and raise the two boys—should be granted custody of them. He was named their legal guardian.

Evans, a Vietnam veteran in his late forties with long, graying blond hair, worked part-time as a sociology instructor and truck-driving teacher at an area community college. After he and Debra's mother were divorced, he later married again and had five children from that marriage. Unfortunately, that marriage also ended in divorce.

Bad luck and tragedy seemed to dog Sam Evans. While he was away in Chicago in August 1996 to receive formal custody of his two grandchildren, his ranch home outside Lawrenceville, Illinois, burned to the ground.

He and the children lived in the Lawrenceville home of Sam Evans's mother for several months while he began the job of building new living quarters near the fire site.

He started with a corrugated tin shed called a pole barn. He nailed two-by-four studs inside, added insulation, and built particleboard walls and a dropped ceiling. He put in carpeting and divided the fifteen foot by forty foot structure into a large kitchen, a den, and Evans's bedroom. There was also a bathroom in one corner and another wall to create a bedroom. There little Jordan shared a bed with Evans's sixteen-year-old boy. Eli slept in another bed in the room.

For a while Evans cooked their meals on a hot plate, until his church gave them a new stove. Furnishings included a large color television set and a stereo.

It was a modest but comfortable living quarters for the small family.

When Jordan and Elijah came to live with him, Evans returned to church after an extended absence and started taking the boys to church regularly. Debra had been taking Jordan and the other children to church shortly before her death, seeking to return to her once happy Christian life.

Going to church, Jordan seemed comfortable in a familiar activity again.

More than a year had passed since the murders. Jordan, almost three years old, was more stabilized. At first he had been in a traumatic emotional state, waking up screaming from nightmares.

In the days shortly after the tragedy, he would say things like "the men shot mommy and killed Samantha, and the lady cut mommy's tummy open and took the baby out," one relative said.

Sam Evans discovered that Jordan remembered Elijah crying for the first time, and his mother lying there, and his sister screaming.

In the early stages of the investigation, Addison detectives interviewed Jordan but decided he probably was too young to testify as a witness.

Jordan was making progress, but he still awoke crying from bad dreams.

One night he left his bed sobbing loudly and walked down a hallway where Evans picked him up and carried him back to bed. Later, when Evans got up again to check on Jordan, he found him standing quietly by Elijah's crib, gently stroking his little brother's arm.

Jordan told his grandfather that he was watching the baby because "bad people" had shot his mommy and taken his brother.

More than once, Evans discovered that Jordan had gotten in bed with Elijah and was sleeping with his arm around him. And often the wide-eyed Jordan would ask his grandfather, "Those bad guys are in jail, right, Grandpa? They're not going to take Eli again, are they?"

As time passed, Jordan was adjusting slowly. Pizza had become one of his favorite foods, and he enjoyed playing electronic and other games, especially with Elijah.

Relatives noticed that Elijah's bubbly personality was remindful of his mother when she was that age. From all signs, he was growing into a normal and happy child.

The grief of Debra's mother at times was overwhelming. Over the months she suffered a weight loss of seventy pounds. Once when Jordan was playing with other children, she noticed he would pretend to shoot them.

"Even when he's playing, they talk about it," she recalled. "They're so young, they don't understand the concept. They'll say something that puts a knife in my heart. They'll pretend they shoot somebody, just like Debbie got shot."

The family had problems observing Eli's birthday on the same date of the murders of his mother, sister, and older brother.

In 1997, two years after the murders, the family waited one week after the dreadful date before giving a birthday party for Elijah. Eli excitedly blew out the candles on his cake and eagerly opened his presents.

One time Jordan asked his grandfather where the rest of his family went.

Evans tried to explain that Jordan's mother, brother, and sister were with Jesus. The boy put on his coat and said he wanted to go live with them in Heaven.

At Christmas when a Christmas tree was set up and decorated, a family member put an angel on top of the tree. Jordan asked if his mother had a set of wings.

At times when he was by himself, Sam Evans had to let loose and cry and kick rocks and walk to the far end of his property to vent his pent-up feelings.

By 1998 the two little boys seemed on the way to more normal lives. They were surrounded by family photos and toys. On one wall of their home was a painting of the Resurrection, the work of Eli's great-grandfather. The cherished painting had been on a shelf, but when the boys came, Evans dusted off the religious art and gave it prominent display.

Sam Evans himself found comfort and hope in the scene of life after death.

* * *

Three other children moved into a new home as well.

Annette Williams's two daughters, ages ten and twelve, and her son, fourteen, were placed in the custody of their mother's former husband, Gary Williams.

Coop County judge Timothy Szwed in making the custody decision said that the ex-husband was fit and willing to take the children.

The father and children were ordered to attend group and individual counseling sessions until the trial of Annette Williams began, hopefully to prepare them better for that family ordeal.

It still would be many months before the first trial started. When the judge made his ruling, it was thought the trials might begin sooner.

The transfer of the children to the murder suspect's former spouse was supported by both the Cook County State Attorney's Office and a private counseling service that had been working with the children over the past several months.

Meanwhile, the lawyers for Annette Williams filed another pretrial motion with Judge Dockery, this one asking for an examination of Williams by a professional psychiatrist to determine if she was mentally fit for trial.

The defendant's attorneys claimed that Williams was not cooperating in her defense. In the motion the lawyers declared that Williams "refused to discuss certain aspects of the case" with the defense attorneys, that she had trouble communicating with them, and that during their discussions "she switches into discussions of fanciful defenses."

Williams later underwent mental evaluation and officials announced that she was mentally fit to stand trial.

Had the accused killer been found mentally unfit, she could have avoided trial and been confined to a mental health facility until she was considered capable of being tried on the indictments against her.

NINETEEN

A mountain of paper files was getting bigger every day as the state attorney prosecutors worked toward the opening trial of Annette Williams, who would be the first of the defendants to be tried.

John Kinsella, Jeff Kendall, and Mike Wolfe were using a large room on the fourth floor to do their preparation work. The room, which was accessible by a small elevator from within the office suite, soon became known as the "War Room."

It afforded plenty of work room, had large tables over which files could be spread, and was away from the daily office traffic and interruptions. Only the prosecutors had keys to the room, which was kept locked when not in use.

Kinsella and his co-prosecutors were of the old school of organizing for a trial. But they knew something more than the usual scribbling and outlining on yellow legal pads was called for in this case. Already the War Room was running over with box after box of evidence; also hundreds of police reports from as many as fifteen law enforcement agencies that had worked on the investigation. The huge discovery file contained witness statements, countless photographs, forensic reports, fingerprint cards, and reports. There were growing stacks of pretrial motions, court rulings, and other legal documents.

It soon became clear that prosecutors would be hard-pressed to sort through the massive amount of material and locate what they were looking for.

"Here we were, three guys of the old school who might scribble a note on a scrap of paper and stick it in our pockets," Kendall recalled.

Luckily, they came up with a solution to locate, as needed, any item from the large volume of material: a young law intern named Elizabeth Ekl who was skilled in computer technology. She drew the assignment of putting the overrunning heap of information on a computer disk. There it would be indexed and cross-indexed, every name of police investigators, witnesses, and potential witnesses—every name that was in the bursting-at-the-seams discovery file, over one thousand names.

Ekl started to work on the giant task in the summer of 1997. She had been given a month and a half free of other office duties to study for her bar exam and to put together the mammoth data file. She worked relentlessly on computerizing the Evans murder case during the day and attended law classes at night. Beth Ekl was a pretty, twenty-six-year-old intern who started as a law clerk in the State Attorney's Office in 1996. Her birth place was Lawrence, Kansas, but her family moved to the Chicago area where she grew up. She became interested in becoming an attorney when she was in junior high school. She went to law school at DePaul University in Chicago and attended night classes while she worked days in the State Attorney's Office.

Classifying everything in a computer was an ongoing

process that continued up to and into the Annette Williams trial and the later trials of the other defendants.

Ekl's computer went with her into the courtrooms, where at the punch of a key or two she could bring up whatever the attorneys needed. It was like having a huge research library at their fingertips.

There was a special section on evidence. The elaborate data file contained the page number in the discovery file where every piece of evidence was listed and briefly summarized and in which one of the many boxes it could be found. All witnesses and their potential testimony were listed by page number.

Before it was over, all of the trial data would not fit onto one disk.

In the War Room the catalogued boxes of evidence were stored for easy accessibility.

Numerous planning conferences were held in the War Room, with trial material spread over the tables. At one such meeting, about sixty attorneys and investigating officers were there. Step-by-step the parts they would play in the trials were mapped out.

Getting ready for the trial, police officers and prosecutors traveled to several different states to interview witnesses and take depositions.

Meanwhile, Beth Ekl took her law exam and became a full-fledged lawyer in November 1997. She would be among the prosecutors seated at the counsel tables during all of the trials. Besides the computer work, she also wrote trial motions.

To the other state attorneys, it was like having a talking combination dictionary-directory of everything in the giant case file immediately available for smooth handling of witnesses and evidence.

As the calendar moved toward March 1998, when Williams's trial date was finally set, the prosecuting staff was comparable to a major strike force primed with all needed weapons and supplies and a War Room plan aimed at getting guilty verdicts.

The tedious nit-picking of countless points of law in a series of seemingly unending pretrial hearings was frustrating to the Evans family, whose members had hoped the trials would be over by now, and they could move on with their lives. Sam Evans summed it up for the victims' family.

"We would like to see it get taken care of as soon after the first of January [1998] as possible. For us, it's unfinished business. It's like going to a funeral and having it never end."

But the intricacies of the pursuit of law must have its day. In fact, day after day after day, it was beginning to seem that way to the families of both the victims and the defendants.

By December 1997, relatives on both sides had stopped attending the pretrial hearings.

Yet, January 1998 brought still another pretrial hearing, with one big difference that would fill the relatives' reserved section of the courtroom for a change.

Annette Williams, who had made no public statement up to this time, would take the witness chair to testify as a witness in a defense hearing seeking to have her signed confession thrown out even before the start of her murder trial.

Taking the witness chair, Williams denied that she confessed to the crimes, in spite of the handwritten statement she had signed page by page on November 18, 1995.

Williams testified she was tired and could not focus during the police interrogation because she was coming off a "cocaine high" during the early hours of the probe when she was in custody.

She admitted that she signed a seven-page confession, but now said she had not looked at the papers before signing them.

"I have a habit of signing things without looking at them," she said.

She testified about being handcuffed for fourteen hours and refusing to eat anything in the Addison Police Station. She later was taken to a lunchroom where she was handed the statement to sign, she said.

Under a fierce cross-examination by Kinsella, Williams denied telling the police that she and her boyfriend, Caffey, used a small silver automatic to shoot Debra Evans. Nor had she told anyone that she furnished the knife with which Joshua was stabbed, or that the newborn baby was hers.

She added, "I don't remember saying any of that stuff, but I was high and anything is possible."

About her and Caffey's arrest at the Schaumburg town house, Williams said that she and her boyfriend had been away only ten to twenty minutes before coming back and being arrested.

"Fedell is a drug dealer, and he was dropping

something off," she testified. Just a quick little delivery of crack and then back. The state called witnesses to confirm that Williams had been advised of all her legal rights and had voluntarily given the confession to assistant state attorney Tom Epach who took it down in longhand. She had signed and dated each page of the statement.

The following day Judge Dockery announced he would not throw out the confession.

The judge said in declaring his decision to admit the confession, "The events as she related them are highly incredible."

He told Williams, "You did make the statement voluntarily and of your own free will. You were not pressured by officers or events, and you were not threatened by officers."

He added, "She understood the Miranda warnings discussed with her those times, and I am not persuaded by claims of mental illness."

One of Williams's defense lawyers, assistant public defender Elizabeth Reed, commented after the ruling, "You don't live in the real world if you don't believe some force or coercion exists in such a police department setting."

The preliminary date for Williams's trial to begin was set at February 17, 1998, by Judge Dockery.

But the selection of a jury to try Annette Williams did not start until March 2, 1998.

The jury selection began in the largest courtroom on the fourth floor of the Judicial Office Facility, before Du-Page County Circuit judge Peter Dockery.

More than four hundred county residents had been

notified by the County Jury Commission to report as potential jurors. About 150 of those summoned showed up, and from them 100 were taken for questioning in groups of 25 as prospective jurors.

The jury panel appeared to be equally divided between men and women.

Twelve jurors and four alternates would be chosen. Judge Dockery started the proceedings by reading to the jury panel the indictments against Williams. He then recited a list of more than fifty possible witnesses who would testify in the trial.

The attorneys had hoped that the sixteen jurors and alternates could be picked in a week, but by Friday the panel still was not completed. It appeared the opening arguments of the long-awaited trial could not get under way until at least the next Tuesday.

The trial was expected to last two or three weeks.

Meanwhile, Sam Evans planned to attend the trial, but he knew that the long absence from work would make it impossible for him to keep his teaching job.

"For Debbie's sake, I feel like I'm responsible, and it's important for me to be at the trials," he told a reporter.

He said that "somewhere down the road" as Jordan and Elijah got older, he would have to tell them about what happened. He said he wanted to be able to tell them that he saw it through, that someone was there representing their mom. "We all want to go and be there at the trials as much as we can."

TWENTY

The big courtroom on the fourth floor, the largest courtroom in the criminal court division, was filled to capacity. Spectators began arriving early to get a seat.

Special sections had been cordoned off for the large contingent of reporters and cameramen drawn to the already widely publicized trial. There was also a reserved section for the Evans family and one for relatives of Williams's.

Illinois has had its share of murder-trial notoriety and learned from experience that guidelines for media coverage are beneficial. Joseph Birkett, state attorney, and Daniel J. Amati, the deputy court administrator, had worked out media controls for the Williams trial.

They included a courthouse media room for daytime interviews and equipment storage, but no telephone hookups were available. A press office with phones was provided in the Government Administration Building across the street.

All photographing, recording, televising, or broadcasting was prohibited above the first floor of the court building. No interviews would be permitted that would block public halls, elevators, escalators, or doorways.

The newspeople were allowed to enter the east door on the first floor without going through the usual electronic screening. Access to the west part of the building would require security checking.

Amati described the purpose of the restrictions as "to make sure all litigants receive fair treatment in an appropriate judicial atmosphere" and that the media and public were accommodated "to the best of the court's ability during trial proceedings."

As always in such situations, some members of the press had less optimistic views about the media guidelines.

The jury of six men and six women filed into the jury box shortly before 1:30 P.M. on Wednesday, March 11, 1998.

Seated at the counsel table were Joseph E. Birkett, state attorney; first assistant Kinsella; and assistant state attorneys Wolfe, Kendall, and Ekl.

Representing Annette Williams were public defenders Stephen W. Baker, Jeanine F. Tobin, and Elizabeth I. Reed.

Judge Peter J. Dockery was presiding.

After the reading of the indictment against her, Williams entered a plea of not guilty. Prosecutor Wolfe walked over to the jury box to give the state's opening argument.

"Elijah Evans was born on November 16, 1995," Wolfe quietly began. "And as he was taken from his mother, his mother was forever taken from him. Within moments of his arrival . . . his older sister was brutally murdered. During his first day among us, one of his two older brothers was poisoned, strangled, and savagely murdered and dumped in an alley.

"How did these hellish acts come to be and who is responsible? That is what this trial is about."

Some jurors and spectators were tearful after the lawyer's words about the children.

Wolfe set the scene for the jury, describing in detail the apartment and the apartment complex where Debra Evans lived with her boyfriend, James Edwards, and her three children. He said Evans was pregnant with her fourth child, who would be named Elijah James after her boyfriend, James.

"Just a few miles away, the defendant—who happened to be a good friend of Debbie Evans's—she, too, began telling people that she was pregnant. Jacqueline Annette Williams. Everyone knew her by Annette. She would go up to her friends and say, 'Feel my midsection. Feel if you can get a kick.' She even had a baby shower thrown for her. She collected baby clothes, car seats, and bouncers."

Wolfe pointed out the two women had much in common—both lived with boyfriends, both had three children.

"And both were preparing for the arrival of a fourth child," said Wolfe. "The only problem for Debbie Evans was that Annette Williams was not carrying a baby. She was carrying a plot—a plot to get a light-skinned baby boy, exactly what was growing inside of Debbie Evans."

* * *

The prosecutor told the jury of the Evans family's last quiet dinner together, of Edwards going to work at his industrial plant job, of him returning home early Friday morning and discovering the horrible, bloody murders in the apartment.

After describing the butchered body of the mother, Wolfe turned to the murder of her daughter. "When sixty-six-pound Samantha Evans slipped into her Pocahontas nightshirt and crawled into her Barbie sleeping bag that night, she had no idea that her baby brother's entry into this world would mean her violent exit.

"That little girl put up a fight, but it was not a fair fight. She had two separate defense wounds on her arms. And her arms and her hands were covered in blood. Her neck had been stabbed repeatedly. . . . Seven times. There wasn't a room in this home that was untouched by this storm of violence.

"It was even more horrible because Joshua and Elijah were missing."

Wolfe related details of the intensive murder investigation. As the search for Joshua and the missing infant continued, "the biggest break came about noon the next day from a very unlikely source," said Wolfe.

"You will meet him. His name is Dwight Pruitt. To say the very least, Mr. Pruitt is very streetwise. He's a member of the Vice Lords street gang. At the time he made a call to police . . . he was on parole for armed robbery."

Wolfe reported Pruitt currently was in the state

prison after pleading guilty to a weapons offense just the previous summer.

"But what he did was the right thing. And it probably was the first time he had ever called the police in his life."

Wolfe told the jurors they would hear the story of Pruitt and his girlfriend, Patrice Scott, and the terrifying ordeal of a seven-year-old courageous little boy, Joshua Evans.

The jury would hear for themselves, through two witness, the dead little boy's words that identified the killers of his mother and sister.

Wolfe outlined the evidence that pointed to Annette Williams as a merciless killer.

He described Annette Williams's motive that prompted the murders, quoting part of her signed confession:

"For our entire relationship together, my boyfriend Fedell has been trying to get me pregnant so that he could have a baby boy. For the longest time he has told me he has two requirements for our child together—that we have a boy and that it be light-skinned so that it resembles him."

Wolfe paused before his final words:

"As you sit in your chairs there, you are sitting across the room from one of the last faces that Debbie, Samantha, and Joshua looked into before they were destroyed. At the end of this case, you will make her face responsible for those brutal murders and kidnapping.

"Find her guilty. Speak the truth."

The skillful argument left many in the courtroom in tears as Wolfe described the cruel deaths.

* * *

Starting his opening argument, public defender Stephen Baker made what at first hearing was a startling statement. He agreed that the state attorney's opening remarks "in terms of facts and physical evidence" were true.

It was not so surprising after his next words indicated the tact the defense would take.

"What complicates this case are the conclusions one draws from them," said Baker.

He went on to explain, "Some parts of the evidence you'll see are clear, the brutality of the murders committed physically by Laverne Ward and Fedell Caffey as described by Mr. Wolfe, why these things happened.

"Miss Williams's level of responsibility is what is in front of you."

Further along in his statement, Baker blamed Williams's involvement in the murders on her "twisted dependence upon Fedell Caffey, the last in a series of ne'er-do-well criminals that she associated with after being married, herself a dropout from high school, one child out of wedlock, two in wedlock, divorced, then she's staying, hanging around with the Maywood crowd, ending up with the likes, the murderous likes of Fedell Caffey.

"She wants a child. In some bizarre thinking on her part, that she could keep a man like Fedell Caffey faithful to her by the acquisition of a child that was not hers, no man on earth can understand that, or woman. But that was the mind-set."

Baker said Evans and Williams were sometimes

friends, "they lived together for a short time in the past."

Then Baker put the spotlight on Ward, the cousin of Williams's. The defense attorney described Evans's relationship with Ward as "physically violent, separation, come back, hot and cold.

"He didn't pay child support. Sometimes he didn't bring over the diapers. Sometimes . . . they would stay together for a week, and it was lovey-dovey again until something happened between the two of them and he would leave. He didn't like the way she was raising Jordan [his child], for whatever reason. Wouldn't let him visit as much as he wanted, gave him grief because he didn't pay."

Baker stressed that Williams told people she was pregnant even prior to Evans's conception of Elijah.

"Why? To get people to be nice to her, to do favors for her. The twisted dependence that you'll see as a theme throughout this trial—not only with Jacqueline Annette Williams, but sadly [too], with reference to Debra Evans whose family, friends, total strangers, would have prayed she would have cut off with Laverne Ward and ended it forever."

Baker turned to Williams's statement to the police that she had come out of the bathroom of the Addison apartment and saw Evans on the floor.

"Can you imagine the horror of a mother of three herself seeing an acquaintance friend on the floor with her head shot and her stomach being essentially gutted by Fedell Caffey who picks up the child, and either because he thought the child was dead or didn't like the color, throws it to the ground like a piece of trash, a theme sadly to be repeated the next day with Joshua Evans?

"Jacqueline Williams, for whatever she is, picked up the child, breathed life into that child.

"Her initial instincts, maternal."

Baker also brought up the words of Williams in her purported confession that Joshua Evans voluntarily accompanied her when she left the death apartment.

"She is going out the door with young Joshua . . . because he knew her, because he trusted her, because she—he did not see her kill his loving mother and sister. He wouldn't have left with her otherwise."

Summing up, Baker said, "But the evidence as you hear it and see it is both clear and unclear. . . . This case is not only about terror, torture. It's about inexplicable behavior. Over the next couple of weeks, you're going to be confronted with horrific pictures of violence and inconsistent pictures about why, and premeditation, and who did what."

A brief pause, and then Baker concluded, "You have a tough task."

The first witness called by the state was James Edwards.

He described the violent horrors he saw after coming home that early Friday morning. His emotional and almost disoriented phone call to the 911 operator was admitted as evidence and played in full to the jury.

Written transcripts of the sometimes incomprehensible phone conversation were furnished to jurors so they could better follow the recorded 911 call.

Part of Edwards's testimony from the witness stand

seemed to confirm the defense contention that Evans and Ward often had difficulties.

Edwards had mentioned he and Debra Evans moved from where they lived in Hanover to Addison early in 1994.

"When you were moving from Hanover Park to Addison, did you say anything to Debbie about that move?" the prosecutor, Kendall, asked.

"Yeah."

"What did you talk to her about, or what did you tell her in terms of your moving?"

"Not to tell Laverne where we were moving because she had had herself a few problems, so if you don't tell him we're moving out, you won't have any problem."

On the second day of the trial, two witnesses testified that Williams had told them at different times she was pregnant. One witness was the county probation officer whom Williams told she had had a baby and was going to marry his father, her boyfriend, Fedell Caffey.

The other was Tina Martin, her sister, whom she phoned early on November 17, 1995, and told that her baby had been born.

Martin recalled saying, "Are you joking me?"

She related she saw by her caller screening that Williams was calling from the home of her friend Betty Larson.

"I said, 'No, you didn't,' and she said, 'Yeah, I did,' " Martin tearfully testified. Williams later said she had given birth to the baby at the friend's house, the saddened witness said.

Martin related that she and her mother drove to Larson's house after receiving the call from Annette about 3:30 A.M. on November 17. Martin testified that she looked at the baby and, still skeptical, she said to Annette, "But he's so light."

Martin said she looked at her sister's friend, Larson, who also had been expecting a baby, and repeated, "He's so light. Are you sure he's not *your* baby?"

Williams told her sister that all her children "were light when they were first born."

Martin also testified that her mother called the hospitals later that same day and could find no record of a baby being born to Annette Williams.

Later that night Martin led the detectives who questioned her and were looking for her sister to the Schaumburg town house where Williams and Caffey lived.

That had been a heartbreaking day for Tina Martin, as was this day. She had had no choice but to testify to information that would go against the sister she loved.

TWENTY-ONE

The birth of Elijah Evans had been scheduled to happen on November 20, 1995.

Debra Evans's gynecologist, Dr. Christopher Olson, testified he had decided to induce the birth because of the history of Joshua Evans, who weighed nine pounds, seven ounces when born.

Because of that, the next baby, Jordan, had been an induced birth to prevent him from getting too large and possibly becoming an obstetric problem. The same procedure was planned for Elijah, Olson said.

The doctor scheduled Debra Evans to enter the hospital Sunday, November 19, to have the baby on Monday morning. A special medicine would be administered Sunday to help soften the cervix; then a contraction medicine would be given the next morning to induce the birth.

Evans also had requested that a tubal ligation be done after Elijah's birth.

Laying a foundation for some questions in relation to the terrible butchering of Evans by her killers, attorney Kinsella asked the doctor to explain what a C-section is and why it is done.

Olson answered, "Cesarean section is making an in-

cision on the mother's stomach, or abdomen, to deliver
the baby if the baby is too big, or if the baby is upside
down or breech, or if the baby is in trouble during
labor—we do a cesarean section for those reasons."

Olson said there are two places to make the incision.
"One of the common areas is the bikini incision, made
in a curved or traversed fashion on the lower part of
the stomach. The other way is the up and down, or
midline, what we use for emergencies when we need
to get in quickly."

Kinsella asked about performing such an operation
if a woman were in an accident and not breathing, or
on the verge of death or, in fact, had died.

"You only have a few minutes to get the child in
that situation," said Olson. "Four or five minutes for
an adult and two or three minutes more for a child.
Beyond that, you would expect the child would not survive birth."

Kinsella asked, "If the mother's heart stops, how
does that affect the survivability of the child?"

"Clearly, you have to get blood [carrying oxygen] to
the area," Olson explained. "If the heart stops beating,
then the blood is not getting there, however well the
oxygen level may be. So you have to have an intact
pump and you need to have oxygen via the lungs getting there as well. So those two things are required."

Because of various muscles and organs inside that
get in the way, three people are needed to accomplish
the delivery in an appropriate manner, said the doctor.
"It takes two doctors and an assistant who will pass
instruments."

In the case of Evans, the horizontal cutting open of

her stomach had "left cuts in the muscles that we usually try to separate and avoid, which would also lead to a tremendous amount of bleeding," Olson related.

"And there was also injury to the intestines, which is also something we avoid," he added.

"How much bleeding would you expect to see from such an injury?" asked Kinsella.

"She would lose several liters of blood."

"And these are fairly substantial arteries or veins that they cut into?"

"Yes."

"That [the blood] would be spurting out?"

"Correct."

Referring now to crime scene photographs, Kinsella asked, "Do these appear to represent a large volume of blood spraying up toward Debbie's face, where she is laying on the floor, up on the couch and onto her face?"

"Yes."

Defense attorney Baker began cross-examination of the witness.

"Doctor, would you agree with the statement that death is a process that doesn't happen instantaneously, where everything shuts down?" Baker asked.

"Correct."

Prefacing his question with the fact that Evans had been shot in the head, Baker asked, "Do you know . . . whether the beating of the heart would have stopped automatically?"

"I don't know for a fact."

"Okay, so it is conceivable that an individual could be shot in the back of the head and yet the heart beat for some period of time thereafter?"

"Correct."

The doctor said that the heart itself has the ability to pump without the need for the brain for a period of time.

The blood that sprayed on Evans's face and a nearby couch indicated her heart was pumping when her abdomen was sliced open, but Olson said he could not say whether she was conscious when the incision was made.

The mother's continued blood flow could have helped the baby survive the crude delivery, even if Evans were dying.

About the blood spray, Baker asked, "It also could have been caused by someone flicking their fingers repeatedly, is that a fair statement?"

"Yes."

"Doctor, in terms of the blood spatter evidence, you're not a forensic pathologist, is that correct?"

"Correct."

"Have you ever studied blood spatter or blood spray patterns in the context of a crime scene analysis?"

"No."

The next day Williams's signed seven-page confession to the triple slayings was introduced through the testimony of Tom Epach, the former assistant state attorney in DuPage County and now head of the criminal division of the Cook County State Attorney's Office.

Epach said Williams gave several versions of how she came to be in possession of the newborn baby when arrested at her Schaumburg residence. The signed confession was given on November 18 during questioning at the Addison Police Department, Epach said.

The confession was read to the jury.

The detailed bloodstain work done by Addison Police Department evidence technicians at the crime scene and the subsequent testing of these blood samples by the Illinois State Police Crime Lab added to the state's growing evidence against Williams.

Kerra Bettisborth, a DuPage County Sheriff's Department employee in the DuPage County crime lab, testified she examined all the evidence from the murder scene that contained possible bloodstains, along with whole blood samples taken from the victims and suspects in the case.

She had processed the stains and forwarded all of the samples to the Illinois State Police Forensic Science System in Springfield.

The county crime lab does not do DNA testing, she said.

The witness testified she also sent blood samples from Debra Evans, Samantha Evans, Joshua Evans, Jordan Evans, Elijah Evans, James Edwards, and the accused killers Annette Williams, Fedell Caffey, and Laverne Ward.

She had determined that human blood was on the poultry shears, the bathroom vanity, an Ace bandage, the vehicle emissions inspection notice, the back stairwell of the Evans apartment, the white electrical cord with which Joshua had been choked, Edwards's Grambling jacket, the bottom of a baby lotion bottle, a blue baby sleeper, and the carpeting from the back of the suspects' Mercury Sable.

She found that human blood also was on a bedsheet found in the street and a piece of gauze and two pieces of tape removed from Elijah.

The witness said examination of the rusty butcher knife found in the dishwasher tray at the Schaumburg town house revealed no bloodstains. (It apparently had been washed in the dishwasher.)

The multicolored scarf reportedly tied around Joshua's mouth in the laundry room of the town house tested negative for bloodstains, but saliva stains on the scarf were submitted for DNA testing.

The mystique of DNA technology was described to the jury by William E. Frank, DNA research coordinator for the Illinois State Police Bureau of Forensic Sciences.

He worked in the bureau's research and development lab. He explained DNA analysis is a series of established techniques used in the forensic biology laboratory to help identify the possible sources of body fluid samples such as blood, saliva, semen, and sweat that may be found at the scene of a crime.

Using a semen sample from Laverne Ward, the scientist had determined that Ward was the father of both Jordan and Elijah Evans.

Said Frank: "The DNA typing of both Jordan and

Elijah Evans are the same DNA type. Both of them show one character that is consistent with the DNA profile of Laverne Ward. Tests showed that James Edwards was excluded as the father of the boys.

"It would be unlikely that any other person but Laverne Ward would be the father of Elijah Evans or Jordan Evans," said Frank. "Ninety-nine-point-nine [99.9%] of the population could be excluded."

Frank also testified the DNA testing on the white electrical cord matched Joshua Evans's DNA. The DNA profile found in the bloodstains on the bathroom vanity top was that of Elijah Evans.

The DNA type on the Grambling jacket stolen from James Edwards and worn by Fedell Caffey on the night of his arrest was a "complicated mixture of several individuals." Elijah and Jordan Evans's DNA were included in that mixture.

Another witness, Kristine Boster, a state lab employee, testified that blood on the poultry shears was that of Samantha Evans. Blood on the carpeting from the Mercury Sable matched the DNA of Joshua Evans, she said.

The DNA in the bloodstains on the bedsheet also matched that of Joshua.

The DNA on the blue baby sleeper found in the garbage at the Schaumburg town house and on a baby lotion bottle from there matched that of Elijah Evans.

TWENTY-TWO

Forensic sergeant Raymond Wojcik knew fingerprints like a medical lab technician knows all those little squiggles in various bodily specimens. But there was one big difference in the two fields.

Out of the hundreds upon hundreds of fingerprints Wojcik might examine, no two would be identical unless they came from the same finger. To anyone who stops and thinks of the millions of people with fingerprints, that identification statistic is mind-boggling.

Wojcik had been with the DuPage County Sheriff's Department for over twenty-two years. He had been assigned to the forensic section of the county crime lab since December 1982.

His job was to detect, preserve, compare, and evaluate latent fingerprint evidence. He was well trained for his mission, having received special training with the FBI and the Illinois State Police. He was thoroughly indoctrinated in the Automated Fingerprint Identification System—the AFIS. This is an acronym, he says, that is a misnomer.

"The system doesn't really identify anything," Wojcik testified when he took the witness chair. "It's an investigative school that allows us to enter unidentified latent prints to run a check through known standards, the fingerprint cards that have been put in there previously. It makes a comparison and develops a candidate list that is examined by the fingerprint examiner."

Besides his in-depth fingerprint knowledge, Wojcik has a B.S. degree in psychology and a master's degree in law enforcement administration.

It was to Sergeant Wojcik and his partner, forensic sergeant Paul T. Sahs, that all the fingerprint evidence from the Evans apartment and the Schaumburg town house was submitted for identification.

Wojcik pointed out the permanency of fingerprints. "They begin to form in human beings approximately the twelfth week of gestation and they last until decomposition." Or amputation.

The big problem is finding identifiable prints at a crime scene.

In the Evans homicides, well over two hundred fingerprints, photographs of fingerprints, and pieces of physical evidence needing to be examined by special techniques not available in the field were submitted to the county's forensic lab.

The first submission was the pair of bloodstained black-handled poultry shears, along with a fingerprint standard card of Laverne Ward for comparison.

Wojcik found no latent prints on the shears that could be developed.

"It's possible to handle an item and not leave an impression that is suitable for comparison," Wojcik said.

Wojcik said he could find no suitable impressions on the iodine bottle recovered from Betty Larson's garbage pile. Numerous physical items and latent print lifts from the Addison apartment—over 150 in all—bore no identifiable prints except those of the Evans family members. From fifty-eight items out of the Schaumburg town house, the print experts identified only three latent prints of Williams, none of Caffey.

But People's Exhibit No. 184 was a different story. It was the State of Illinois vehicle emissions test notice Detective Van Stedum found on the hutch that appeared to have a bloody print on the right bottom corner.

Wojcik said he used a chemical reagent to process the piece of paper. The fingerprint expert explained that on a porous surface like paper, the print would be absorbed and could not be dusted with powder and lifted.

Instead, the chemical inhydrent was used to get the print. The tested item is sprayed or dipped in the chemical, hung up to dry, or ironed out very gently with steam, or put in a humidity cabinet. Protein is one of the human elements in sweat that leaves a fingerprint.

After the chemical clearly brought out a print on the emissions notice, Wojcik had taken a photograph to preserve the image.

"After developing those negatives and making sure the image was retained, I did a side-by-side comparison with the image I developed on the emissions notice to the fingerprints standard card files that were submitted in regards to that submission."

Wojcik said he matched the fingerprint to the right index finger of the card bearing the name Jacqueline Annette Williams.

To better demonstrate his findings to the jury, Wojcik

had prepared a chart showing an enlarged photo of the print on the emissions notice and another enlarged photo of the right index fingerprint of Williams from her standard card.

"What I have done for demonstration purposes is to mark the corresponding ridge events on each finger—the corresponding ridge event on the latent print to the fingerprint standards," Wojcik explained.

He detailed the method further to the transfixed jurors: "First thing we look at when making identification is the fact that there are prints similar in shape, are the patterns similar? Obviously, if they are totally different, we are not going to waste our time looking at that.

"In this particular case we have the general shape of the print. What we are looking at is this area here, commonly known as the core of the fingerprint. As you can see, there is a general resemblance in the shape.

"But that's not enough for identification. What we have to do is go in and look at the individual ridge events. As I mentioned, these ridges are not smooth and continuous, but they are broken. You can see we have a ridge that comes up and divides. We have a ridge that comes down and ends.

"Those ridge events, are they consistent to a sufficient degree of similarity in these fingerprints? We all have these ridge events, but their arrangement is unique to the individual."

But Wojcik warned, "Although the prints originate from the same individual, you can have distortion in there. You can have heavy pressure. It's up to the skill of the latent fingerprint examiner to determine if these fingerprints are similar."

Wojcik added that in addition to all the fundamental precautions, once the identification is made, another examiner has to verify that work. "That's our protocol, our policy of assurance."

The examiner had identified fifteen similarities in each of the compared prints, far above what is enough to confirm identification.

"It's my opinion that these two prints have sufficient degree of similarity that they were made by one and the same individual."

That individual was Annette Williams, who literally had left her calling card in blood at the crime scene.

"There are other ridge events in there that correspond, but for demonstrative purposes I just stopped at fifteen."

Wojcik said no latent prints were developed on the white cord used in the attempt to strangle Joshua Evans.

Also, no prints were developed on the butcher knife thought to be the murder weapon.

Four latent prints found in the murder apartment were never identified. Wojcik said they were submitted to the FBI, which also could not make any identification.

On cross-examination, Baker asked, "Is it correct to say that, in general, you cannot tell the age of a fingerprint?"

Wojcik replied, "In general, what you are saying is true. It's extremely difficult to time-date a fingerprint."

"So, with reference to the latents off the emissions

notice, that could have been put on there a day, a week before, a month before, you don't know?"

Wojcik said, "I would have no knowledge when that print was put on there."

Baker had one more question: "Sergeant, with reference to the unidentified latents from the Addison apartment that were sent to the FBI . . . , do you recall what they were taken off of by chance?"

Wojcik thought for a few seconds. "Yes, I do. Let's see, one was an impression that was taken from the top edge of the TV. One was from a Southern Grove peanut butter jar. One was from a Jewell brand cherry soda can, and one was a latent print removed from a carton of cigarettes."

TWENTY-THREE

When getting ready for trial, the prosecutors realized some of their witnesses were the kinds of people who usually would be found testifying for the other side. At this point in Williams's trial, the pivotal testimony on which the state's case probably would stand or fall would come from two people whom the defense was certain to try to discredit.

Taking the witness chair first was Dwight Pruitt, twenty-six. He gave his address as the Illinois Department of Corrections in Chicago. He said he was confined there after conviction on a weapons charge. Nor was it his first time behind bars. In the past he also had been convicted of armed robbery and before that for possession of a controlled substance.

Pruitt testified he was a member of the Vice Lords, known among lawmen as one of the Chicago area's toughest street gangs. Pruitt admitted to having been a member for fourteen years.

In November 1995, Pruitt said, he was living with Patrice Scott, two stepdaughters and the six-week-old daughter he had by Scott. They resided in an apartment in Villa Park, Illinois. At that time he was on parole from a six-year prison sentence for armed robbery received in 1992. His arrest for possession of a controlled substance occurred before then, he said.

He was not a man that anyone would expect to voluntarily call the police.

Pruitt related the hard time he had locating a telephone to notify the police on that November 17 after he recognized the missing Joshua Evans's picture on a TV newscast. It was the little boy that Annette Williams had dropped off at their apartment about 1:00 A.M. that day, saying his mother had been shot in a drug deal that went bad.

The weeping boy had told Pruitt and Scott over and over that night and the next morning that his mother and sister had been killed by Williams, Caffey, and Ward. He had repeated the accusations in front of Williams, words that prompted the painful iodine poisoning, attempted strangling with a cord, and finally the fatal stabbing of Joshua in the back of the car.

Pruitt testified that Williams, after being confronted by Scott with what Joshua said, angrily told the boy to "shut his fucking mouth," to which the sobbing boy had cried, "No! No! No! You know what happened! You were there!"

Now, through Pruitt, the shocked jury heard Joshua's emotional and spontaneous outcries that identified the murderers.

Pruitt was cross-examined by defense attorney Elizabeth I. Reed. The following is a portion of that cross-examination.

Reed: "Part of the conversation that Joshua said, you got from Patrice, didn't you?"

Pruitt: "Everything I heard came from the boy's mouth."

Reed: "Well, for instance, you were not present in Schaumburg, right?"

Pruitt: "Right."

Reed: "So if she told anything that happened in Schaumburg, you knew it because she told you, right?"

Pruitt: "No. When I found out about Schaumburg, it was when the detectives arrived. I didn't know what happened in Schaumburg."

Reed: "So you went to call the police before Patrice told you what happened?"

Pruitt: "I told the police on the sole strength of what the little boy told me and what I heard on the TV."

Reed: "When Patrice came back with Annette and without Joshua, Patrice didn't tell you anything . . . about what happened to Joshua?"

Pruitt: "No."

Reed: "You heard Joshua say four black men came into my bedroom window?"

Pruitt: "No, he said four burglars."

Reed: "Do you remember any other description Joshua gave of the four burglars?"

Pruitt: "He named them. He named the people that was at the house."

Reed: "And the fourth person he named was something like Bo or Boo Boo, a nickname?"

Pruitt: "Right."

Reed: "Now, Joshua did not run from Annette in your house, did he?"

Pruitt: "No."

Reed: "He did not pull away from her and try not to leave with her the next day, did he?"

Pruitt: "I can't say. I don't know. I wasn't standing in the living room with them. I was in the bedroom when they left . . . the apartment."

Pruitt: "Now, your testimony was that Joshua was saying these things at five or six in the morning, does that sound right?"

Pruitt: "Probably so, yes."

Reed: "Patrice and Alexis [Pruitt's baby daughter] went with Annette anyway, right?"

Pruitt: "Yes, from my understanding they both went to Wal-Mart."

Reed: "Is that where she told you they were going?"

Pruitt: "Yes, to Wal-Mart and to drop him [Joshua] off at his auntie's house or something like that."

Pruitt said he was in the apartment when Patrice talked to some officers after she returned. The police had come in response to Pruitt's phone call.

"They were trying to talk to her, but she really didn't want to talk," Pruitt testified. "She was kind of hysterical at the time. I was trying to get her to talk. I was getting mad at her because she wouldn't tell them where they took the little boy. They wanted to know where they took the little boy, and she was crazy, you know, frantic, hysterical. She wasn't saying any audible words you could make out.

"Then they asked her if she would take them where they took the little boy, and she said she would try to remember which way they went."

Pruitt said he accompanied Scott and the officers when they left in a police car to search for the location.

Prosecutors thought Pruitt had weathered well the penetrating cross-exam by the attorney Reed. Although he couldn't relate every event to an exact by-the-clock time, he knew what he had heard and he was not shaken in his testimony. He did not budge.

They speculated that one phrase Pruitt had spoken in his phone call to the police would be remembered by the jury above anything else. Pruitt had said it with an undeniable conviction of truth in his voice.

"Somebody's lying, and it ain't that little boy!" Pruitt had told the police dispatcher.

Pruitt might be a prison-hardened con, but one thing was apparent in his testimony. That grieving, terrified little seven-year-old boy's words had touched his heart.

The woman who took the witness stand next was obviously nervous. Patrice Scott, Pruitt's thirty-year-old live-in girlfriend, was about to tell of the horrifying events she had witnessed on November 17, the last terrifying hours in Joshua Evans's life that ended with his brutal murder.

She was well aware that Annette Williams's lawyers would try during their questioning to discredit her as a witness, hoping to damage her testimony through which Joshua Evans's incriminating statements would reach the jury.

It was 10:00 A.M. on March 18, 1995, the seventh and last day of testimony in the Williams trial. The jury was brought in and Scott was sworn in as a witness.

Prosecutor Michael Wolfe began his questioning of the state's key witness. Asked to identify the defendant, Scott pointed toward Williams, who was wearing a gray suit.

Frequently in tears as she testified, Scott related the nightmarish events that began early that Friday morning, when Annette Williams dropped Joshua Evans by the apartment that Scott and Pruitt shared.

She told the jury of Joshua's whimpering and crying the rest of that night, of his repeated statements that his mother and sister had been killed by "Annette, Fedell, and Laverne," of Williams's anger when she came back later that morning and was asked by Scott about the boy's accusations.

She testified about Annette making Joshua drink from a bottle of iodine, of his throwing up, of taking her six-week-old baby and going with Williams to see her supposedly newborn infant.

She tearfully described the attempted strangling of Joshua in the laundry room by Williams and Caffey that stopped when Scott screamed and shoved Williams away from the boy; of Williams bringing the rusty butcher knife and giving it to Caffey; of being in the gray Mercury Sable and seeing Caffey raise the knife and plunge it into the boy in the back being held down on the floor by Williams; of feeling Joshua kick against the front seat as he was stabbed; of the boy being dumped in the Maywood alley.

She tearfully related Caffey's threats to kill her and her children if she told anyone what happened; of Caffey getting out of the car and Williams driving her and her baby home. And how she led the police to where Joshua had been thrown in an alley.

She was sobbing as the direct examination by Wolfe was finished.

Defense attorney Baker rose and said, "Given her emotional state, it may be appropriate to take a few minutes."

A five-minute recess was called by the judge, and a bailiff brought a glass of water to the upset witness.

Court reconvened and Baker started his cross-examination of Scott, a portion of which follows:

After Scott said that Williams asked her to accompany her to the Schaumburg town house and to the store, Baker asked, "And you went with her?"

Scott: "Yes."

Baker: "And you knew that there was some kind of problem between Joshua and Annette?"

Scott: "I went. I didn't really think we would be in the danger that we were in. She was my friend."

Baker: "I take it you regret ever getting into the car?"

Scott: "I regret the whole thing from the first day."

Scott said that they stopped at a grocery store for her to get cigarettes. Williams bought a soda pop, and returning to the car, she poured some of it into a cup for Joshua and he drank it.

Scott was asked if she saw another black man talking with Fedell Caffey in the laundry room when she first arrived and passed the room as she went upstairs.

Baker: "And is that an individual you know to be Bo Carlton?"

Scott: "I never saw Bo. . . . I did not see Bo in the apartment."

Baker, handing the witness several photographs: "I show you a photo array. Do you recall ever seeing this?"

Scott: "Yes."

Baker: "And do you know an individual named Bo Carlton who is among those six pictures?"

Scott: "Yes."

Baker: "And which number is he, please?"

Scott: "Three."

Baker: "And was this shown to you by a detective from Addison named Vrchota?"

Scott: "Yes."

Baker: "And did you identify Bo Carlton as the individual who was present at the Schaumburg town house?"

Scott: "He looked like [him]. [But] It wasn't Bo."

Baker: "Did you tell police officers that the individual you knew as Bo threatened to kill you?"

Scott: "It wasn't Bo. I don't remember telling them that."

Baker: "Was there a black man at the Schaumburg town house other than Fedell Caffey who threatened to kill you?"

Scott: "Fedell Caffey is the only one who threatened me."

Baker: "So you never told any police officer that you overheard a conversation among Fedell, Annette, and Bo Carlton where he said, 'Kill you.' "

Scott: "Fedell Caffey threatened me. I never said Bo Carlton was in the house."

Baker: "I take it Miss Williams never threatened to kill you?"

Scott: "No . . . it was Fedell . . . more than once."

Baker: "You were terrified for your life?"

Scott: "I was afraid for my life and my baby's life and Joshua, too, for the record."

Baker: "You did what you were told because you were afraid?"

Scott: "Yes."

Baker: "How many times did Fedell Caffey stab Joshua in the car that you saw or heard?"

Scott: "I only saw once when I looked back once."

Baker: "And you recall a kick to the back of the seat?"

Scott: "Like kicking the seat. A little person, wasn't a big kick, you know, just—"

Baker: "A little kick?"

Scott: "Not a little kick. What I am saying is a little person kicking. I know it was Joshua."

Baker: "And you kept your eyes straight ahead?"

Scott: "Yes."

Baker: "Because you were afraid for your life and the life of your child?"

Scott: "I was afraid."

Baker: "Miss Scott, with regard to the strangling of Joshua in the—was that in the laundry room of the town house in Schaumburg?"

Scott: "Yes."

Baker: "You screamed. You pushed Miss Williams, and she dropped the rope and eventually threw it to the ground, is that correct?"

Scott: "They let it go."

Baker: "And is that when Fedell told her to get the knife?"

Scott: "No."

Baker: "So she just showed up with the knife?"

Scott: "She went upstairs. She left . . . the room."

Baker: "And did she give the knife to Fedell?"

Scott: "She put it on the bed [in the laundry room] after I screamed. . . . I don't know what she was going to do with it, but she put it on the bed."

Baker: "She placed the knife on the bed?"

Scott: "No, she just had it out. When she pulled it from behind her back, she just had it out."

Baker: "But I thought you just said she placed it on the bed?"

Scott: "And that's what she did with it."

Baker: "Miss Scott, if you don't understand my questions, indicate that to me, and I will rephrase them, please. Are you with me there?"

Scott: "If you can't understand my answers, then give me time to say them and you will understand them."

Baker: "After Miss Williams dropped you off at your home . . . you were aware that Dwight Pruitt had called the police?"

Scott: "He didn't call the police when she dropped me off. It was after she dropped me off."

Baker: "You and Dwight Pruitt talked about what happened before he called the police?"

Scott: "I told him what happened in the apartment, yes, and then he told me to lock the door. He was going to call the police."

Baker: ". . . Eventually a uniformed Villa Park police officer arrived at your apartment area?"

Scott: "Yes."

Baker: "Do you remember what you told him?"

Scott: "The story."

Baker: "Do you remember telling him that you and Miss Williams dropped off Joshua in Maywood?"

Scott: "That is a lie. We weren't alone."

Baker: "Initially to the police officers, did you tell them that you and Miss Williams dropped Joshua off in Maywood?"

Scott: "I do not remember telling them that, but I do remember waiting later to tell them about

Fedell because I was afraid. He had threatened me and my children."

Baker: "He threatened to kill you and your children if you talked?"

Scott: "Correct. . . . Until I felt that . . . that I would be safe and my family and that we would get help and be protected, then I gave his name."

Baker: "Do you remember telling the police that two men—this is Joshua talking to you—two men climbed through a bedroom window?"

Scott: "Four burglars. When you are upset in the beginning, you know, of something like that, and you are talking, sometimes you are hysterical and stuff, but I remember Joshua telling me four burglars. I don't remember saying four men."

Baker: "Do you recall making the statement to them [the police] that Annette told you that Fedell had wanted Annette to take Josh to the south side but that she, Annette, had told Fedell that the child would get hurt?"

Scott: "No, sir."

Baker: "Would a review of the report refresh your recollection?"

Scott: "Yes." (She was handed a report to read).

Baker: "You reviewed that report, is that correct?"

Scott: "I reviewed the report, but I don't remember saying it like that."

Baker: "How do you remember saying it, about the child would get hurt?"

Scott: "She said that he told her to take him to the projects out south and dump him off, and I said, 'Why? He would get hurt. Let's take him to the police station, so they can find his family.' "

Baker: "So you ended up at the store and then the Schaumburg town house?"

Scott: "She wanted to go by and stop and pick up her baby. I thought eventually we would get there [the police station]. I wasn't driving."

Baker: "In the course of your various conversations with the police, were you told that Miss Williams said you had an end of the cord in the car on the way to Maywood?"

Scott: "I was told that."

Baker: "And you denied that?"

Scott: "It's not true."

The state rested its case following Scott's testimony. Surprisingly, the defense called only five witnesses.

A twenty-six-year-old female friend of Annette Williams testified that Williams had faked being pregnant before 1995.

"It's a female game we used to have," the woman said. "You say you're pregnant to keep the guy."

However, the witness said that she thought Williams was telling the truth about being pregnant in 1995. She said that Williams even had a baby shower, at which friends and family members played a game trying to guess the weight of the baby. She also had received baby gifts.

Michael Simo, a police detective, testified that Scott in her initial talks with investigators had mentioned the name Bo Carlton as a man she had seen talking to Caffey at the Schaumburg town house when she arrived there with Williams and before Joshua was killed.

The detective recalled Scott told him that Bo threatened to harm her if she talked to police. It was the name that Scott in her testimony had denied mentioning to police, adding if she had, she was mistaken.

The detective also testified that Scott told him in the early stage of the probe that she did not know who held Joshua when Caffey stabbed him to death.

Addison detective Cathy Vrchota testified that two months after the murders, Scott identified the fourth "unknown" burglar as Bo in a police lineup and said that Bo had threatened her, and she feared he would come after her.

Addison detective Joe Lullo related that Scott, when first telling of Joshua's description of the killers, said that "four black men" had entered the apartment.

Detectives said Carlton, a distant relative of Williams's, was checked out thoroughly, and no reason was found to charge him. The identity of the fourth "burglar," if there was a fourth person, remained a mystery.

The defense wrapped up its testimony in about an hour.

Williams was advised by Judge Dockery that she had a right to testify if she so chose, but Williams did not take the stand.

The defense rested. Closing arguments were set for the next morning.

TWENTY-FOUR

The closing arguments of the attorneys were heard on Friday, March 20, 1998. This is the time that lawyers call upon their oratorical skills, but more importantly, their ability to sum up the facts concisely and effectively for a jury that has listened to many witnesses.

Judge Dockery made a short statement of his own.

"As I indicated to you yesterday, the evidence in this case has been completed. The attorneys have the opportunity now to engage in closing arguments before you. Closing arguments are the opportunities the attorneys have to discuss with you the facts and circumstances of their case and reasonable inferences to be drawn from those facts and circumstances.

"Like opening statements, however, closing arguments are not evidence. And if any statement is made by an attorney that is not based upon the evidence, you must disregard that argument."

Assistant state attorney Kendall rose to speak first for the prosecution.

"Good morning, ladies and gentlemen.

" 'Somebody's lying, and it ain't that little boy.'

"Dwight Pruitt heard the truth. He heard what Joshua Evans said, and he heard what the defendant said. And for the first time in his life, he picked up the phone and did the right thing.

"He called the police because he had heard the truth. *Somebody is lying, and it ain't that little boy.* Joshua spoke the truth.

"What else did you hear from Patrice [Scott] and Dwight? Lock the doors. What did Josh say? Lock the doors. The burglars know where I am. They might be coming to get me. Little Josh couldn't have spoken truer words, because, sure enough, the burglar came back and got him. And then, unfortunately for little Josh, it meant his death.

"In this case Joshua Evans has spoken to you from the grave through Patrice and Dwight, and he has told you about the who, when, why, where of the murders of his mother, of his sister, and of himself. And in those statements he named to you his murderer and murderers, Annette, Fedell, and Verne. That little boy had talked the truth from the grave.

"See, somebody is lying, and it ain't that little boy."

Kendall declared that Williams's involvement in the crime was overwhelming. "This trial was about one thing, her desire to take from the womb of Debbie Evans what she couldn't have, and that was Elijah Evans. . . . But for her desire to have that, the Evans family would still be alive."

He reminded the jurors that the first thing Williams said when arrested in Schaumburg with the newborn infant in her arms was, "That's my baby!"

"That's what this case is all about. The slaughter of a family for her desire to have the unborn child of Debbie Evans."

He said, "These horrific crimes are an Annette Williams production. She picked the day the mother, daughter, and son would die. Isn't it amazing how death follows this woman around during this trial? She goes to Addison, [ ] Swift, Apartment [ ], and two people in there are butchered. She goes to Villa Park and picks up a little boy and takes him to his slaughter that happens in Schaumburg, at her house. She drives to Maywood, and they find a dead, mutilated little seven-year-old boy in an alley there.

"My God, everywhere she goes, death is following her."

Kendall summarized the evidence against Williams found in the death apartment: the bloody Ace bandage and "a big, old fat fingerprint on a bloodied emissions notice."

Kendall pounded away at the evidence involving the defendant: the bloody sheet found only blocks from where Joshua's body was dumped, the matching sheet in Williams's upstairs bedroom, the white cord with Josh's blood on it found in her garage.

Kendall addressed the circumstantial evidence found in Williams's town house that tied her to the crimes: a discharge information notice for the baby, with a little blue bow and its height and weight and circumference of its head; a phony birth certificate; baby clothes in her closet still with the tags on them; one baby lotion bottle with Elijah's blood on it.

"You are going to hear about accountability—meaning that a person is legally responsible for the conduct of another person when either before or during the commission of the offense, and with the intent to promote and facilitate the commission of the offense, she knowingly solicits, aids or abets, or agrees to aid, or attempts to aid the other persons in the planning or commission of the offense."

That in itself nailed Williams to the murders, the prosecutor argued.

"Let's think about this," he said. "Asking for a gun, finding out when James Edwards wouldn't be home, going with two other people—one who has a gun—because Debbie Evans is shot in the head, to a house where the baby is stolen from. Of course, she is involved before, during, and after. This is an Annette Williams production. But for her, all these people would still be alive.

"Aggravated kidnapping. Our youngest victim in the history of the world . . . it is aggravated kidnapping when she leaves with those two children from [Evans's apartment]."

Kendall said that Williams was guilty—because of her involvement, her being the basis of the plan. "She is guilty whether Verne Ward did the stabbing, whether Fedell did the stabbing, whether any of the combination did the killings in those apartments, because she's accountable for their conduct.

"Samantha Evans was killed because they were going to steal this baby. They were in the course of committing . . . aggravated kidnapping. It doesn't matter who killed her.

"When a tornado hits a house and kills everybody

inside, you don't ask which wind killed who. The tornado, Team Williams, killed Samantha Evans, and she's responsible for her first-degree murder.

"Joshua Evans died a horrible death. And how is she responsible? From her first reaction. It is unbelievable. Let's see what she does to contribute to his death. What do they find in the garbage can? Well, an iodine bottle because she tried to poison him. When that wasn't good enough, she went back to where Fedell was.

"What else did she do to little Josh? Wrapped a cord around his neck. He was fighting for his life. Strangled him. Little Josh was tough. He wouldn't die and that was a problem for them. That's what she told the police in her statement.

"Lastly, what does Fedell tell her to do? Get me a knife. What do you think she's thinking when she goes upstairs to get this knife? Fedell is going to peel some oranges?

"According to Patrice . . . [Williams] holds that little boy as Fedell butchers the life out of him."

Referring to Williams's confession, Kendall said her claim of "going to the bathroom at the moment in time when everybody is killed" is nonsense. "She's trying to talk her way out of murder."

Speaking of the crime scene pictures of the victims, Kendall told the jury "in these pictures, in their death, you see the defendant Annette Williams."

A collage of family pictures and the crime scene and autopsy photos of them had been displayed for the jury during the trial. The gruesome photos had caused some of the jurors to break into tears and hug each other.

"You see her face in those pictures, and the enormous evil that created this macabre collage is over-whelming, and that evil is sitting right here in this courtroom. But, fortunately, the evidence in this case is overwhelming of her responsibility for these horrific crimes. From these photos, the Evans family is collectively screaming out for you to do justice in this case.

"Let the defendant know by the verdicts you sign that somebody was lying, and it wasn't that little boy.

"Sign those guilty verdicts."

Defense attorney Jeanine F. Tobin next spoke to the jury.

"When you were questioned as jurors, you remember we asked you about your possibly being very much overcome and upset about the . . . circumstances of this case, and we asked you if you could hold those in abeyance until the completion of the case and keep an open mind," Tobin said.

"I know it is difficult after what you have seen and what you have heard, but I am asking you to do that in fairness to the defendant."

Tobin said she would explain to the jury "why Annette is here today and what her role is in this entire tragedy. Words cannot express the horror of what happened to these three young people in Addison almost two and one half years ago. . . . The victims are in the cold ground and the state is asking you for justice. It is going to be your duty to decide where justice is properly going to be placed.

"I ask you, ladies and gentlemen, what kind of an animal would have done these things. Only someone in ome sort of vicious, uncontrollable, crazy, maniacal age could have committed the crimes of this heinous ature, and you are being asked by the state to say that nnette Williams did these. I suggest that is not so.

"What happened that night we won't ever really now for sure. There are a lot of unanswered questions, ut one thing we do know if you believe the defendant's confession. . . . She went to the bathroom. She eard a shot, and we don't know how long she was in he bathroom.

"She heard a ringing sound and she runs out. She uns into the living room, and what does she see? She ees her friend, Debra Evans, lying on the living room loor, being gutted, being gutted! What she saw is what ou see in some of these pictures.

". . . Now I suggest to you that Annette Williams tepped into violence beyond any control that she had. suggest to you that she did not know what to do. Vhat she had been ordered to do and had been ordered o do for all their relationship is to do what Fedell vanted her to do.

"I suggest also that when Patrice Scott testified—and he told that she was in fear of her life because of hreats of Fedell Caffey to her—that the same thing pplied to Annette Williams.

"Annette Williams and Patrice Scott were in that car, nd they did the things that they did because they were old to do them, and they were afraid for themselves nd their own families.

"The state does not have forensic evidence tying Annette to anything. What they have is her statement saying I was there in Addison."

The defense lawyer argued that Williams did not kill Debra or Samantha and that her instinct was to protect Joshua. "He ran to her. If she was one of the 'bad men,' he would never have run to her. He knew her . . . trusted her."

Tobin attacked the testimony of Patrice Scott, accusing her of trying to hide her role in those events; the attorney pointed to purported discrepancies in Scott's earlier and later statements to detectives.

"Annette Williams may have a lot of defects, but she is not an evil person," Tobin told the jury. "She got caught up in a twisted relationship. . . . She was an unwilling participant.

"She's caught up in a crazy relationship, a relationship of desperation, a relationship of fear," said Tobin. "Annette Williams may be guilty of many things, but she is not a murderer."

The defense contended that Williams was an unwilling participant in the crimes because of her fear of Caffey and her obsession to please him in his wish for a light-skinned boy baby.

She also saved baby Elijah's life by breathing into his mouth after Caffey had removed the baby and tossed it on the floor, the defense reminded the jury.

TWENTY-FIVE

It was up to John Kinsella, the lead prosecutor, to put the final touches on the state's case, giving the final closing argument. He was well aware that his words would be the last ones the jury would hear before going to the jury room to deliberate.

He talked about the attorney's tools: words.

Speaking in even tones, Kinsella began: "The problem is in this case they don't really work because none of those words really make the connection with the facts of this case, really convey what's happened here. But yet as lawyers, like any other trade, we have to continue to work with the tools we have. So doubtless to say, there aren't any tools to adequately work this case, to explain how something like this could happen."

He had their full attention now, their eyes fixed on him as he moved slowly along the jury railing.

"You know, counsel said the defendant is not an animal—and I assure you this was not done by animals. That's what makes this so hellish. This was done by human beings, and in the past two weeks, that has been shown to you in this case.

"But as lawyers we have to work with these words, even in a case . . . that would give nightmares to

Stephen King. This is unimaginable, what happened here."

He said the crimes committed "would be hard for decent, reasonable, intelligent, articulate people to understand," and for him to put that into words would shed light on what was "macabre and evil circumstances."

"Yet, through your experience and your common sense, you have to, and that's part of what the instructions are going to tell you to do—to try to climb inside her mind and use reason in an unreasonable person, use logic in an illogical person—but you have to do that."

Kinsella, a veteran of courtroom battles, is a seasoned and confident speaker. He needed few notes because he had lived this case for some two and a half years. The horror of it had etched the details in his mind.

"So you look at what she did, and in response to what you just heard a few minutes ago [Tobin's closing argument], ask yourself certain questions about what was going on in the defendant's mind at certain points and time."

Referring to testimony that Williams had faked being pregnant for a long time, even before 1995, the state attorney said, "This nonsense about faking pregnancy in the past has nothing to do with this case."

Turning to James Edwards's testimony that Williams had questioned him about his work schedule a week before the murders, Kinsella said, "Counsel says forget the conversation with James Edwards. But who did she talk to? Why would she ask him those questions?

"According to what you just heard, she was just interested in talking to Debbie. She wasn't talking to Debbie. She was talking to James Edwards, and she wanted to know what James Edwards is doing, when he goes, where he is, when he gets back. Why? What thought was in her head that caused her to think to ask those questions?

"What was going on in her mind when she talked to Darlene Bearden. That's something you have to reconcile together with all the other evidence in this case. She told this woman, a total and credible county employee, that she had given birth to a baby named Elijah [before the murders happened], gave her a preview of the crime to come, which suggests perhaps she is not very bright. What she does is illogical and unreasonable, but that's the way her mind works.

"Out of *her* mouth, not Fedell Caffey, not Laverne Ward, she said one significant word: Elijah. No one had gotten into her head when she said that. Fedell Caffey wasn't there. What is going on in her mind when she tells Darlene Bearden and mentioned this name Elijah. And in a case such at this, in any case, what you do is look at all the pieces, not as individual pieces. . . .

"So you say to yourself, you ask yourself, what is going on in her mind weeks or months before this happened. You put together those facts with her asking about guns, together with telling people she's pregnant, together with telling Darlene Bearden she had a baby named Elijah."

Kinsella continued: "Now what is going on in the hours before this happens? Who was she meeting with?

Verne Ward. It is suggested to you that, well, it's just a coincidence she's meeting with Verne Ward. It's just a coincidence that Verne Ward is looking for her. They're cousins, after all.

"Just a coincidence. What you heard here is the suggestion of a lot of coincidences, one that would make her the unluckiest woman in the world. What a coincidence she happened to be in Debbie Evans's living room when her boyfriend cuts the baby out of her, and she happens to have bought baby clothes and had a baby shower, a woman who wasn't pregnant planning to have a baby. What a coincidence.

"She goes around telling her entire world I'm pregnant and having a baby. Who do you think was motivated to cut that baby out of Debbie Evans? Do you think it was Fedell Caffey? Who told her entire universe that she was having a baby? The defendant."

Kinsella turned to the seven-page statement Williams had given to the police. "They keep referring to the seven-page statement, her confession. You have heard us refer to it as her *final* version.

"You need not accept her final version as the truth. You need not do that. You can use your common sense. Look at all the other evidence. You put it all together and you start looking.

"What else was going on in her mind at various times inside that apartment? Each of you in examining this evidence ask yourself who had the most to gain by getting this baby? Who had told everyone in her family and her world that she was having this baby? Who was the most motivated to get the baby? Use your common sense and ask yourself those questions. Then ask yourself the final question, 'Do I believe she was in the bathroom?' I submit to you from all the evidence in this case that you look at everything, certainly her claim 'I was in the bathroom.'

"I believe the only reasonable inference from all the evidence, direct and circumstantial, is she put her hands up inside the woman's abdomen and pulled the baby out. She did. There is no reason, based upon common sense and logic and the evidence in this case, to believe otherwise because she said she didn't do it.

"Fedell did it. I just stood and watched. I just stood and waited. And then I'm the savior. [Referring to testimony of Williams blowing into the newborn's mouth and starting him breathing] That is insulting. She saved the baby? She stole the baby. Someone steals your car, you don't thank them for saving your car, do you?

"Now, what is going on inside her head when she's in the apartment? What is going on inside her head when she leaves that apartment with the baby—and here's a point I want to touch on right now. It has been suggested again, based on her statement, that Joshua came out of hiding and grabbed onto Annette because he recognized her, and Annette is his savior and protector who says that is the way it happens.

"Is that what Patrice Scott described? She said Joshua Evans said he was hiding and after Williams left, he came running out.

"He didn't run into his protector. He ran into his executioner.

"So this suggestion of Joshua [running to her] was to help her convince you that she's innocent. What does she do to protect and care for Joshua? She killed his mother, killed his sister, then killed him.

"It has been suggested to you that you somehow should view the actions and statements of Joshua as evidence of her innocence. That's absurd, absurd. The person who held him as he was being stabbed and strangled and tried to poison him. What is going on inside her head?

"This nonsense about him coming to her and clinging on her and vomiting. The vomiting she's talking about happened at Patrice's house. You heard what Patrice said, she tried to poison him and the kid vomited.

"So you don't have to accept her version. Ask yourself if she is trying to minimize her responsibility when she talked to the police. Of course she did. She did it from the moment they started talking to her.

"But she didn't break down and say, 'Yes, I wanted that baby, I had to leave with that baby, I wasn't leaving that apartment without that baby and, yes, I took some scissors and knives and ripped Debbie's belly open. Took the baby out.' Because she didn't say that means it didn't happen? You have seen the pictures. It did happen. This isn't a hypothetical situation we're talking about here. It happened.

"Someone did it. It has even been suggested that it would probably take more than one person to do it. But certainly someone did it, someone motivated to do the most indescribably horrid thing you could probably imagine.

"What type of motivation does that take? What type of desire? What type of blind objective must she have to say I'm walking out of this apartment with a baby whether I have to cut it out or not?

"Ask yourself, who had that type of motivation here? The only reasonable inference is Annette Williams. What is going on inside of her head when she drops this boy off at Villa Park? She can't bring him home, her kids are there. She has to do something with him. She goes to a friend. She gives her friend a line, and the story line, something you hear a lot about in this case, is Annette Williams.

"So she lies and leaves the boy there. What is going on inside her head? She decided she's going to follow through with—what? What she started months earlier. The baby? Yes, it is stupid. Yes, it is illogical. Yes, it is indescribable that people's minds would work this way, but it happens."

The persistent prosecutor spotlighted Williams's record of not telling the truth. "You heard her sister say she called and said, 'Here, it's my baby. I had a baby. We had a baby. Fedell and I have Fedell, Jr. . . .

"She did this, she said this and she meant it. And it is so ridiculous, of course, her own sister and mother didn't believe it. But the fact they didn't believe it doesn't mean that it didn't happen.

"It happened. So what is going on? Is that consistent with what has been going on in her mind: The baby shower to talking to Darlene Bearden to meeting with Verne Ward, going to talk to James Edwards? Look at all the evidence. Does it flow?

"Whenever these sick, stupid thoughts got into their

minds, they got there, whether it was on the doorstep of . . . . Swift or in the living room of . . . . Swift . . . those sick thoughts, intent on her part, it happened, it happened, and you have seen the evidence of it and the pictures of it.

"They want to pretend this didn't occur. She passed this baby off as her own, phony documents and all. Again we get into she's the protector, she's afraid. Please remember evidence comes from the witness stand. Evidence comes from exhibits.

"It has been suggested to you that it is Fedell Caffey pulling all the strings. It was Fedell Caffey that was the main guy, and she has to do what he says. Ask yourself this question: Where is the evidence of that?

"Where is this evidence of fear and fright on the part of Annette Williams toward Fedell Caffey? Zero. Did anyone testify to that? No.

"Is it a reasonable inference to draw from anything? No. Look at all the things she does by herself. She talks to James Edwards. She takes the baby.

"She covers Debbie Evans's body. There's some truth in that statement. I want you to think about that for a minute. Because you remember how Samantha's body was left? Do you remember what he said, James Edwards? Both Debbie and Samantha were covered from head to toe with a blanket.

"Do you think that's a coincidence that Fedell Caffey had the same thought about Samantha as she [Williams] was having about Debbie, or do you think the same person covered up both bodies? Was she in that bedroom with Samantha? Did she cover that body up, too?

I suggest to you she did. Who was the one hovering around the apartment with the baby?

"She picks up Joshua. She alone, Fedell ain't around. She's the first person to attempt to kill Joshua. They want you to say, don't believe that; this is a coincidence; the unluckiest woman in the world.

"She alone gets the knife. Think about that for a minute. You just heard that poor threatened woman, feel sorry for her . . . think about the thoughts going through her mind as she leaves that room, walks up the stairs, goes to the kitchen, finds the knife, walks down the stairs with the knife.

"What does she think the knife is going to be used for? You know exactly what she thought: to kill this little boy. There's no question about that. They suggested the state didn't prove it. What did the police detective tell you? As soon as he looked in the dishwasher, there is no blood on it. A rusty knife in there. What did Dr. Cogan tell you?

"The knife is about an inch wide; the knife has a blade about six or seven inches long. The knife is dull. The little boy was stabbed with a knife an inch wide, seven inches long. They happen to have an old rusty, dull knife like that in the dishwasher.

"That is circumstantial evidence. That is compelling. That is believable. That is the truth.

"The sheet—who gets the sheet? Who has to cover up the bodies? Who runs up and gets the sheet? Use your common sense. Look at all the evidence.

"Ask yourself who was doing things. Who is it more likely, based on the evidence, that did this?

"Who covers up this body to drive into Maywood?

Who picked the place? Who drove into the alley? Who kept the sheet to dump it out the window? She did.

"Remember this Pettaway. They make a big deal that Pettaway somehow is making this up because he has a drug problem. He saw them talking that afternoon. He doesn't know what they were talking about. But do you know what was more interesting? Where does he see Annette again? What is she doing? She's at the car wash, and the real sick part is, she has her daughter cleaning up Joshua's blood out of the back of the car. Who's cleaning up the mess? She's cleaning up Fedell's mess. Fedell does these murders, cuts babies out for her.

"She's cleaning up her own mess."

Kinsella returned to his dominant theme, what motivated the murders of the Evans family members.

"This case is about that baby and if you take one moment of time in your mind, stop and imagine what this case is about.

"About eleven forty-five in the evening when she pulls in the garage with the baby, what exists in that point of time, at that one moment in history, what is taking place? There is Annette with the baby, the proceeds of a theft and a murder. There is Fedell wearing James Edwards's jacket. There is the backseat of the car covered with that little seven-year-old boy's blood. There is a cord laying on the floor in the garage with this little amount of blood from him on it. There are these documents upstairs. There are baby clothes. There is this Baby Magic bottle. There were two DNA types on the bottle. It is Elijah's blood and there is DNA from Jordan. It came from inside the apartment.

"What is going on inside of her mind at that moment in time? Look at everything in your mind's eye. What does that show you?

"She's got the baby, got the blood, we have a motive, we have the proceeds, we have the attempts to cover it up, the documents to show her mother, the motive because she wants the baby.

"Then complete that moment from the first time the police talked to her. There are [four] words in that moment that explain everything in this case: *'This baby is mine.'*

"That's what this case is about.

"Now, in the course of examining what you've just heard from counsel who talked originally a few minutes ago about a child, as if Annette is a child. This is not a child's crime. The crime is about a child, about taking someone else's child, but don't view her as a child. Don't view her as an animal.

"It has been suggested to you that she doesn't look or act like some sick, crazed killer. Do you want to know what crazy killers look like? Just look over there and that's what they look like. They don't have horns coming out of their head. They look like Annette Williams. You *earn* that title. She has earned it."

Suddenly, Williams, glaring at Kinsella, cried, "So have you! You have lied and I am tired of it!"

One of the defense lawyers turned and grabbed Williams by the shoulders and calmed her down. A murmur swept the courtroom. Kinsella had been the object of Williams's obvious anger, and her temper had ignited. Kinsella wondered if the jurors were thinking about another time that Williams was said to have flown into a rage, that time at Joshua Evans, telling him to "shut your damn mouth," as Patrice Scott had testified.

Kinsella did not react to or mention the display of anger from the defendant at the attorneys' table. He moved on with his statement to the jury.

"That little boy was telling the truth. He didn't coach Patrice as to what to say, and she didn't coach him. They related to you what they recalled happening and that is what happened. And this idea that you are to believe just because she [Williams] said it—that Patrice held on to one end of that rope, that cord—I think you believe what Patrice told you, that she was holding her baby, scared for her life. She was the one doing everything she could within reason. Maybe you think she should have done more to try and stop these people from killing that little boy, but Patrice is someone who got wrapped up in something. Why was Patrice taken there? They suggested Annette brought her with her for protection.

"According to what Patrice told you, Dwight was in the other room. They have this conversation. This little boy is telling the whole story in front of Patrice, and Annette is getting mad. She's telling Patrice not to believe it. She doesn't know what to do.

"Remember at that earlier point what they thought they would do? Dump him. Get rid of him. They think Josh didn't know what happened, he didn't know who the killer was. Just dump him in the projects. Let's just get rid of him.

"Once he started saying through Patrice, 'I am a witness! I am a witness!' in front of them, he was going to die. She was going to kill him. That was what was going on, and in your mind you know it. Look what she did. Look what ultimately happened to that little boy.

"And why was Patrice brought along? She heard what Joshua said. Fortunately, she was here today to tell us what Joshua said. But it wasn't any kindness or a sense of protection or fear on the part of Annette Williams. It was because, unlike Josh, she survived.

"It was also suggested to you to not be fooled by evidence. I would suggest to you more importantly, don't be fooled by the lack of evidence or by non-testimony. What your obligation to do is to consider the evidence and the testimony—not what some lawyer comes up here and says is a fact.

"What I'm talking about is this business of Mr. Caffey. It was suggested to you that she's afraid, frightened, and an abused woman who's doing what Fedell wanted. The problem with that is there is no evidence of that. There has been no testimony about that.

"You're at the part in this case now when it's time to go back and deliberate, and what you do is reach a verdict.

"The word verdict derives from the meaning of 'to speak the truth.' When you go back there and deliberate in this case, it is for the purpose of finding the truth and reaching the truth, and remove the view of innocence that no longer suits her.

"Think about this cord being wrapped around this little boy's neck and one end of it in her hand. Think about what Dr. Cogan told you the consequences of this were: Blood filled the face and the capillaries in his face began to burst, and he can't breathe and he's choking and screaming and kicking and fighting for his life. And as his eyes were open and looking about him as his life was being choked out of him, who is the person that he sees through that cord? Whose face is he looking at as he was held?

"You heard the doctor explain Joshua was unconscious or immobilized. The evidence in this case is that he was not unconscious. Patrice told you he was kicking, he was fighting for his life. He was a tough little seven-year-old boy who did not want to die. He was not unconscious.

"Look at Samantha, ten years old. Defense wounds when she was attacked by Verne, Fedell, and Annette, or any one of the three of them, and they are all three guilty of murder, absolutely, as if they plunged those scissors in her neck themselves. What did she do? She fought. She struggled. That little girl fought for her life.

"Obviously, someone wasn't restraining her.

"But Josh with the final stabs, he was immobilized. Who did that? Look at all the evidence: The baby shower, Darlene Bearden, the meeting with Verne, going into the apartment, snatching the baby, the taking of the boy, the lying to her mother, the lying to police—put it all together. Who was holding Joshua? The defendant Annette Williams.

"What was Fedell doing? That dull, rusty knife had to be forced. They had to work to get the knife into that little boy's body, and it didn't even cut the bone. It just scraped against the bones inside of his body.

"That rusty knife, is that something you put in your dishwasher normally? No. You put it in there if you have blood all over it. That rusty knife had to be forced into that little boy's body and all the way through his body into his back. But, just as with this cord, that's the last face he is looking at, that's the person who is responsible for his death—no more, no less than Fedell, no more, no less than Verne.

"The young mother is dead because she [Williams] wanted a light-skinned baby. A cute, innocent little girl is butchered because she probably walked in on Annette Williams's desires. A little ten-year-old boy—I should say he would be ten tomorrow—is dead. They want you to believe or to use Josh as their witness as proof of their kindness.

"That frightened, little, seven-year-old child is dead for only one reason:

"Because he ran into his executioner. He ran into Annette Williams. When you think about the legal responsibility, the factual responsibility, the full responsibility in this case, think about her holding this cord, think about her walking down those stairs with a knife, think about who wanted that baby, think about who dug that baby out of Debbie Evans."

Kinsella spoke firmly. "Don't buy into this final version minimizing her responsibility—this statement to police, as if it is the gospel truth. This cord and all the other evidence tells you the truth, tells you the verdict, tells you what a tough job this was in this case, tells you what you must do when you reach the verdict, when you speak the truth.

"The truth in this case is simple: Annette Williams is a murderer. She murdered Debbie Evans, she took that baby. Whether she plunged those scissors into that little girl's neck, all the way back to her spine, she's just as guilty or responsible for Samantha. No matter who had the sick thought to do that to that little girl. She's guilty.

"And Joshua, it is overwhelming. Her depraved lack of feeling toward that child is just mountainous.

"Do your duty.

"Find the truth.

"Return verdicts of guilty of all counts of murder and aggravated kidnapping.

"Thank you."

The large courtroom was completely silent.

Before too long, the long-waiting families of both the victims and the defendant would know the trial outcome.

The jury filed quietly out of the jury box and into its deliberation room.

The bailiff closed the door after them. Williams also was escorted out of the courtroom to await her fate, now in the hands of six women and six men.

The jury was out only two hours.

Solemn-faced and quiet, the jurors returned to the jury box at 5:00 P.M. on Friday, March 20, 1998.

The judge cautioned the onlookers in the jam-packed courtroom to make no verbal reaction or any other demonstration upon the announcement of the verdict.

Tension filled the courtroom as the large audience, the attorneys, the defendant and her relatives, braced for the reading of the verdict.

The jury foreman turned the verdict paper over to the court clerk.

Then it was announced that Annette Williams had been found guilty of murder and aggravated kidnapping on all six counts.

Williams sat stoically, showing no immediate emotion. Later she would hug her mother who was in tears.

The Evans family members were pleased with the jury's decision.

"Right now, we are feeling good, but we know this is just the first phase," said Sam Evans, Debra's father, when he talked to reporters and TV crews outside the courtroom. "We have two more trials to go."

Debra Evans's sister, Wendy, told a *Chicago Tribune* reporter, "We lost three members of our family, and we will never get them back. How can you expect us not to be overwhelmed with excitement and grief?"

Sam Evans Jr., a brother of Debra, said, "I do want to wish Joshua a happy birthday. He would have been ten tomorrow. I hope he knows that his words are still strong."

The jury returned to court Monday to decide if Williams qualified for the death penalty under the requirements set forth by the Illinois death sentence law and U.S. Supreme Court rulings. But attorneys and the judge were busy working out the complicated instructions the judge would give the jury.

During the presentencing hearing on Tuesday, Judge Dockering instructed the jury about eight specific aggravating factors necessary to assess the death penalty:

more than one person was killed; that the defendant knew or should have known that they would be killed; that the victims were killed during the offense of aggravated kidnapping; that two of the victims were under twelve years of age and were killed with brutality and heinousness reflecting wanton cruelty; and that one victim, Joshua, was killed to keep him from cooperating with the authorities in solving the murders of his mother and sister.

Considering these requirements, there was little doubt in the minds of anyone who had heard the testimony and evidence as to what the jury would do.

After deliberating for one and a half hours, the jury decided the convicted killer and kidnapper was eligible for the death sentence.

Both sides would present testimony in the punishment phase of the trial the next day.

TWENTY-SIX

Sorrow filled the big courtroom.

The family survivors of Debra Evans, Samantha, and Joshua spoke their sad words. They unveiled for the jury the chasm of despair and loss and loneliness left in the wake of the three murders.

Their naked grief was an exhibit laid out for the world to see and for the jurors to decide whether the convicted murderess and kidnapper—who seemed unremorseful, at least judging from her facial expression during the trial—would be put to death or put behind prison walls for the rest of her life. Most of the time, Williams, wearing clothing supplied by her mother and sister, and with her hair cut in a shorter style, appeared to be unaffected by the grisly and emotional testimony from witnesses.

In a brief opening argument on the punishment that Williams should receive, Elizabeth Reed, DuPage County senior public defender, called upon the jurors to "think in terms of justice and not revenge" when they decided on a sentence. She pointed out Williams had led a hard life in her existence among drug dealers and abusive boyfriends.

Reed told the attentive jurors, "We need a reasonable, a moral judgment. She is the mother of three, she was a Girl Scout, she sang in the church choir, she's a sister, she's a daughter, and she was a mother at sixteen."

Debra's sister, Wendy, recited the scars left on the psyche of Jordan Evans, who was only seventeen months old when he walked through the blood and among the bodies for several hours before being found by James Edwards.

"Little Jordan was so frightened when he came to stay with us," Wendy said. "He would run away and curl up in a ball when people he didn't recognize came into the house. Jordan would shake and cry uncontrollably.

"Jordan has reoccurring nightmares of what he saw that night when his mom and sister were brutally killed. Screaming in his sleep, he would sit up with his eyes wide open, reliving the events. . . . The nightmares continue to this day."

Also still having nightmares about the horrible murders was Debra's father, Sam Evans. "This is like a horror movie to me, but it's not a movie, it's real. . . . The pain does not go away. It's still there."

He said it was impossible to describe the "void and empty feelings" that were inside him.

"On a regular basis, I have nightmares of what Debbie and Samantha went through the last moments of their lives. I have constant nightmares of what Joshua went through the last minutes of his short life."

Evans told the jury he is raising Jordan and Elijah. "Thank God Eli lived," Evans said.

But he said it is heartbreaking to come upon Jordan "telling Eli about those bad guys that killed their mom and sister" and adding, "But we're safe now. Grandpa promised he won't let them hurt us."

The tearful Evans turned to the jury and said, "Please help me keep my promise to my grandchildren."

Wendy and her mother, Jacalyn, wrote a statement together, which was read to the jury:

"At the wake for Debbie, Sam, and Josh, the terrible sight of the three coffins in front of me was overwhelming. How do you say good-bye to three beautiful people that you need so desperately in your life to feel complete?"

The sister recalled she said good-bye to Debbie one final time when she threw herself over "Debbie's cold, lifeless body and could not let go.

"I begged her not to leave. My dad and aunt had to pull me off.

"Annette Williams had murdered a part of each one of us," said the statement. "We will never be the same again."

Scott Gilbert, Samantha's father, tearfully related how Samantha had been with him during the summers and holidays at his home in Florida. "This is the one thing I thought I would never do—bury my own daughter. I became extremely depressed, wouldn't talk to anyone, not even my wife."

He said he remained "terrified that what happened to my Sam will happen again. I am constantly looking in on my other daughter to make sure she is safe . . . Like never before in my life, I find myself consumed with grief, loss, and the most destructive emotion of all—hate."

Many of the jurors cried as the Evans family told of their deep grief over the violent deaths of the mother and her two children.

Martha Martin, the heartbroken mother on the other side, described her daughter Annette in earlier years as a good school student and a regular churchgoer. She remembered it was in high school that Annette started changing. No longer did she come home from school on time. She became pregnant and quit school in her sophomore year.

She quit going to church. Her life had been going downhill ever since her last year in high school, the tearful mother recalled.

Yet, Williams was a good mother to her own children and took good care of other children with whom she was a baby-sitter, her mother testified.

"I know she was a better mama than I ever would be," Martha Martin said. "Even since she's been in jail, she calls me to make sure the children have what they need."

Mrs. Martin said she had two of Annette's children, and Williams's ex-husband had one in his care.

Her mother testified, "She can be influenced by a lot of people. She likes to do what other people do."

In line with the defense attorney's portrayal of Williams as an abused woman with a twisted dependence on her boyfriend, Caffey, several police officers called by the defense testified they had investigated instances when Williams was badly beaten by Caffey and former boyfriends.

A female friend of Williams told the jury she had seen Annette with a badly battered, swollen face, one eye nearly closed and her lip cut after a severe beating by Caffey.

The defense also brought in a psychologist, Dr. Cushing, who had interviewed and made various tests on Williams during her confinement in jail.

Ironically, his testimony was helpful to the prosecution, such as when he said that the defendant knew right from wrong at the time of the murders and that she "could have controlled these events."

The psychologist related that during their interviews Williams had strongly denied she was involved in the crimes, even when confronted by the overwhelming evidence that contradicted her denials.

The doctor told the jury Williams refused to take responsibility for her actions, shifting the blame to others.

Moreover, said the defense's doctor, Williams was not psychotic and was not having a psychotic episode during the murders. Another surprise from the defense witness: Williams never told the psychologist she had been threatened or harmed by Caffey.

The doctor said that Williams was "more preoccupied with ridiculous things—like the lack of freedom and privacy in jail—instead of the serious issue of facing the murder and kidnapping charges against her."

But, Williams did suffer from antisocial and bipolar personality disorders, the psychologist said. Her IQ was well below average, too.

Williams suffered from clinical depression, said Cushing, a disorder that made her "psychologically vulnerable to predatory males.

"Threats from such males could cause her to do things she would not initiate," Cushing said.

Under cross-examination the doctor said Williams never showed any remorse over the killings during their jail interviews. She steadfastly denied having any part in the crimes, said Cushing.

The assistant state attorney Jeff Kendall in closing arguments said, "If this is not a crime where the death penalty is appropriate, I don't know what is. The overwhelming magnitude of the crime screams out for death. In this case, the true measure of justice is death. She's the MVP of criminals."

The prosecutor had words for the duty performed by the jury members. He compared their service to that of soldiers serving their country in war.

"But many soldiers in war never saw the horrors that you have seen in this courtroom in this trial."

In final arguments Williams's attorneys acknowledged that she had a part in the killing of Joshua Evans. However, they asked the jury not to impose the death sentence on their client because Ward and Caffey did the other two murders.

Public defender Jeanine Tobin told the jury, "There

is no evidence that says Annette Williams was involved in the killing of Debra Evans. What you have is a seven-page confession and she never indicated that she killed Debra Evans or that she intended to kill Debra Evans. The state is asking you to make great leaps."

Public defender Stephen Baker described the situation faced in the punishment phase of the trial.

He said, "It's a razor we are walking in this courtroom today—between life and death, between distinctions, between roles."

He pointed out to the jury that the state had not provided evidence that Williams killed anyone, and that a sentence of life in prison would be more appropriate than the death sentence.

Ending his closing argument, Baker said loudly, "She has done some terrible things . . . but stabbing Samantha is not one of them! Nor is putting a bullet in Debra Evans's head!"

Prosecutor Kinsella recalled for the jury that Williams had faked being pregnant several months before the murders. He pointed out that Williams in her confession mentioned she wanted a light-skinned baby.

His voice rising sharply, Kinsella declared, "Who had this disgusting motive? Who told everyone in the world that she was having a baby? Who made every conceivable plan to prepare for a newborn?

"This was an Annette Williams production," he concluded.

The verdict did not come as quickly as it had in the guilt or innocence part of the trial.

The jury deliberated four and a half hours before reaching a verdict.

The jury decided that Annette Williams should be put to death for the crimes.

Williams showed no reaction to the death verdict. Members of her family burst into tears.

Debra Evans's mother, although feeling sympathy for Williams's mother and sister, told reporters later, "This doesn't bring back Debra, Samantha, and Joshua, but if this case doesn't deserve the death penalty, what case would? It was the right thing to do."

Talking to reporters later, the jurors agreed that returning the death penalty verdict was relatively easy, as compared to the emotionally trying experience of sitting through the trial and listening to the horrifying testimony.

One twenty-three-year-old male juror said, "I personally thought it was an easy decision. I went in there open-minded, but to see the defendant with absolutely no remorse on her face when the family of the victims gave their impact statements, that really got to me."

But one courtroom observer thought Williams had blinked back tears during the heartrending testimony of the victims' relatives, but was not sure.

A thirty-six-year-old female juror said, "After applying everything we heard, it was clear."

But she said jurors "went through hell. Some of the jurors are still having nightmares. Sometimes these thoughts keep coming through. It was scary."

A nineteen-year-old college student who was on the jury said, "We applied the law to the facts, and the facts to the law, and it fit like a puzzle."

In an interview earlier in the trial, the defendant's tearful mother had said, "There are a lot of pieces to the puzzle missing. She loved people too much. Not just kids, but all people. She is not the monster everyone thinks she is."

Annette Williams became the fourth woman on death row in Illinois.

TWENTY-SEVEN

Laverne Ward, wearing a dark blue suit, sat at the counsel table with his attorney Earl Washington of Chicago. The defendant was quietly scribbling notes on this Monday morning, June 1, 1998, the opening day of his murder trial.

From his appearance he could have been taken for another lawyer sitting at the table. Ward watched as the prosecutor John Kinsella led with the state's opening arguments.

"Ward has the blood of the Evans family all over him," Kinsella said, describing the evidence against the defendant as "overwhelming." Ward's face didn't change expression.

Kinsella ran down the list of past events that pointed to Ward's guilt in the murder of Debra Evans and her daughter, Samantha: Ward had expressed an intent to kill Debra Evans in May 1995; Ward was known to have had an argumentative phone conversation with Debra only hours before the killings; one witness had seen him change from bloody clothing into other garments the night of the murders; and still another witness had told police that on Thursday night Ward tried to sell a portable stereo for crack cocaine on Chicago's west side. It matched the description of the one belonging to Samantha and missing from the Evans apartment.

As in Williams's trial, the state's key witness against Ward would be Patrice Scott, who had overheard Joshua's accusations against Ward, Williams, and Caffey before the boy himself was murdered the next day.

In the defense's opening remarks, Washington said the state had no evidence linking Ward to the apartment crime scene except the testimony of Scott, whom the lawyer considered a questionable witness.

"Laverne was not present—never present—at the taking of anyone's life," Washington told the jury. "He was not there at the home of Debra Evans." The lawyer added that several friends of Ward's would testify that he was with them at various times during the period in which Debra and Samantha were slain.

Not one bit of evidence—blood, fingerprint, or clothing—was found at the scene that would link Ward to the murders, the defense attorney said.

Plus, Ward was in the custody of police when Joshua was stabbed and his body dumped in a Maywood alley.

Ward would take the stand to deny he had any part in the murders, Washington told the jury.

But the prosecutors told the jurors that Ward was the "co-producer" of the murder plot and was one of the three people whom Joshua Evans identified as the killers of his mother and sister.

The prosecutors admitted the only "eyewitness" they had was Joshua Evans, who had identified Ward, Williams, and Caffey as the killers of his mother and sister over and over to Patrice Scott before his own murder.

"Joshua left his brother a legacy," Kinsella said. "Joshua lived long enough to tell who it was that killed his mother and sister."

Patrice Scott was the first witness called by the state. Washington immediately was on his feet to object, saying the prosecution had advised him earlier that three witnesses would be called before Scott, and her being called now took the defense by surprise—not having enough time for preparation of cross-examination.

The judge declared the state was under no obligation to call witnesses in any special order and "calling of the witness can be no surprise to the defense." He denied the request to delay the witness's testimony.

Questioned by ASA Wolfe, she told of the events from Thursday night when Jacqueline Annette Williams dropped off Joshua at Scott's Villa Park apartment; and of the horrendous happenings that took place in Williams's Schaumburg town house, ending finally in the stabbing murder of Joshua.

On cross-examination Earl Washington began a deadly barrage of questions seeking to discredit Scott's shocking testimony. A portion of the cross-examination follows:

Washington: "When you initially spoke to the police, did you tell them that it was you and Annette alone that took Joshua to Maywood?"

Scott: "No."

Washington: "Did you ever tell the police that you and Annette took Joshua to Maywood and that Annette took him someplace out of your sight?"

Scott: "I don't remember saying that."

Washington: "Did you ever tell the police that Laverne Ward was not present at the scene of the crime of Debra Evans?"

Scott: "Can you say that again?"

Washington: "Did you ever tell Detective Valerie Thomas that Laverne Ward was not present at the murders [in the Evans's apartment]?"

Scott said she recalled having a conversation with Thomas, but she did not remember what they talked about.

Referring to Joshua's statements about the killing of his mother and sister, Washington asked: "After he had told you what you had said, did you then call the police?"

Scott: "No."

Washington: "After Joshua had told you about these burglars . . . killing his mother and sister . . . did you at that time attempt to contact police?"

Scott: "No."

Washington: "You had already seen blood on Annette's coat, had you not?"

Scott: "She said she took his mom to the hospital."

Washington: "See if you can see what I'm holding now. Did you see Fedell Caffey and Annette

Williams wrapping this cord around this boy's neck in an attempt to strangle him?"

Scott: "Yes."

Washington: "Did you believe they were trying to kill him?"

Scott: "Yes."

Washington: "Did you then try to call the police?"

Scott: "I couldn't call the police at that time. We couldn't get out of the house."

Washington: "Did you then tell your good friend Annette, I'm leaving here. You are murdering this boy?"

Scott: "I did ask, can we leave?"

Washington: "Did you tell Annette, I will not participate in your attempt to kill this young boy?"

Scott: "There was not a reason to tell her that because I don't feel I did."

Washington: "But you said nothing?"

Scott: "I screamed and I pushed her. . . . When I pushed her, they stopped."

Washington: "Do you know why they were trying to strangle him in the first place?"

Scott: "I guess because he told about what happened. She said he talked too much and he knew their names."

Scott testified that when she and Joshua left in the car with Williams driving and Caffey and Joshua in the backseat, she believed they were taking them home.

Washington: "Is it at this time that you see Fedell stab Joshua in the backseat of the car?"

Scott: "In the garage before we leave."

Washington: "At that time when you claim that you saw Fedell stab him, did you believe that Annette and Fedell were going to kill Joshua?"

Scott: "Yes."

Washington: "Did you at that time leave the vehicle, leave that presence of Fedell and Annette?"

Scott: "You cannot get out of the garage. That's where it happened, in the car in the garage. . . . There was no way out of the garage."

Washington asked the witness if she tried to get out of the car as they drove from the house and then on an expressway. Scott, who said she was holding her baby in her arms, answered, "You mean jump with a two-month-old?"

Washington: "Are you telling the court and jury that the car never stopped for any stop signs or stoplights as it traveled?"

Scott: "I don't remember, but as we was driving, she went to the expressway."

Washington: "When Fedell stabbed him [Joshua] in the garage, you say, did he scream?"

Scott: "I don't remember. I just remember him kicking the seat, kicking the seat."

Washington: "And when they took Joshua out of that car and tried to make him walk to his death, what did you do, Miss Scott?"

Scott: "I was trying to keep my baby quiet. She was screaming and shaking."

Washington: "Your baby knew what was going on?"

Scott: "She was screaming. She wouldn't be quiet."

Washington: "Did you at any time when Fedell and Annette left your sight run from that car screaming for help?"

Scott: "No, I was scared to run. . . ." (She began sobbing and did not finish her reply.)

Washington: "At this time, Miss Scott, you knew they were acting to murder him, didn't you?"

Prosecutor Wolfe objected on grounds Washington asked a question and didn't give the witness an opportunity to answer before he asked another question.

The judge instructed the defense attorney to give the witness time to answer.

"I will withdraw that question and wait for the answer."

When there was no response from Scott, the attorney said, "I have no other questions."

But then he changed his mind. "Pardon me, I think I do have one last question, if I may?"

The judge said, "You may."

"Would you tell the court and jury why you gave Annette Williams materials to help her to clean off the backseat of her car where Fedell, as you say, tried to kill Joshua?" Washington asked.

"She didn't say she was cleaning the backseat of her car. She said she was cleaning the floor where the baby had vomited on it, which I never looked back [at] there. And I wanted to act as normally as possible to get a chance to tell Dwight what happened."

"Did you ever tell the police that she was cleaning the backseat of her car?"

"I don't remember," Scott answered.

Washington said, "I have no further questions."

Breaking into sobs, Scott cried loudly: "If I could have did anything differently, I would have! I couldn't help him! I couldn't! God knows the truth! Joshua knew the truth! And I'm telling the truth as it was told to me! Until you are in my position and went through what I went through, then you judge!" She continued weeping.

Wolfe interrupted. "Could we have her come off the stand, Judge?"

Judge Dockery told Scott, "Yes. Ma'am, you may step down."

He excused the witness, and she continued to cry as she was escorted from the courtroom.

In spite of the defense's hammering questions about whether she had called the police after hearing Joshua's accusing statements, or after the attempts on his life, prosecutors believed that Scott had come across to the jury as a sincere and honest witness who had been too afraid for her baby and herself to do anything until she could get away from the killers.

Reporters cornered some relatives for sidebar comments during breaks in the testimony.

Sam Evans, the father of Debra Evans, said the possibility of a fourth person being involved in the killings still troubled him—Joshua reportedly had mentioned "four burglars" when describing the killers.

"The possibility always has been in the back of my mind," the father told reporter Robert McCoppin of the *Wheaton Daily Herald.* "You can't help wondering if there's somebody out there walking around that was there."

Evans said the second trial had been hard on the family. One reason being that the family particularly blamed Ward because he had abused Debra during their relationship.

"If he and Debbie had never had a relationship, we would still have Debbie and Samantha and Joshua," the bereaved father said.

An uncle of Laverne Ward's told the reporter that he could not believe the charges against his nephew. He said he had helped raise Ward, whose nickname was "Voodoo." He recalled that Laverne and Debra "got along fine" when they visited him during holidays.

"He had more women than most people had clothes," the kinsman said. "That's why I wouldn't understand why he would want to hurt another woman."

TWENTY-EIGHT

What time the murders of Debra and Samantha Evans happened and the whereabouts of Laverne Ward during that time period became the focus of the trial.

At first the homicide investigators had looked at a wide window of time in which the killings could have occurred—any time between when Debra was known to have last talked on her telephone Thursday evening up until James Edwards came home from work and found the bodies.

But the time period was narrowed when Edwards revealed the children usually were in bed by 8:00 P.M. and their mother no later than 10:00 P.M. The children were in their nightclothes, but Debra still had on a sweater, slacks, and underclothing when found.

Those circumstances would indicate the killers struck sometime after 8:00 at night and before 10:00 P.M.

Three witnesses who lived in the apartment complex in November 1995 gave testimony relative to the time that the murders might have happened.

Jackie Sullivan, a resident of a next-door apartment building, testified she had heard a gunshot while she was talking on the phone. She had turned out her lights and looked outside, but saw nothing. The loud report seemed to have come from a northerly direction, toward the area of the Evans apartment.

The witness had heard the shot during her phone conversation, which lasted from 8:30 to 9:30 P.M., but she could not be more exact.

Another apartment resident, Tennie Clay, told the jury she had seen four people talking in the apartment complex parking lot between 9:00 and 9:30 P.M. From her window she had seen a man, wearing a dark hood with a jacket over it, walk over to three other people standing together. She heard the man yell, "I'm going to do something."

"And then he lowered his voice," she related.

She said one man was shorter than the others and one was much taller. Ward is short, standing about five feet four inches. She could not identify Ward as being the short man she saw or any of the others. One man in the group looked like a light-skinned African American, the witness said, a description that sounded like Caffey.

On cross-examination the witness said she did not see whether any of the group had weapons, what they did next, or where they went.

The question of when the murders occurred was raised again by the testimony of Gayle Jensen, a resident who lived below the Evans apartment. Jensen said she heard "sounds" in the Evans apartment above her at about 9:40 P.M.

"There was a very hard thump or thud that would have been on the floor of that apartment," she testified. Investigators later told her the spot she indicated was where Evans had fallen.

The state presented over the next week a string of witnesses who testified about Debra's past encounters with Ward.

Scott Gilbert testified he once had been in Debra Evans's apartment to visit Samantha when Laverne Ward kicked in the door. Gilbert also recalled that two days before her murder Evans asked him to take the children if anything happened to her.

Washington asked for a mistrial on grounds that Gilbert's testimony about Ward kicking in the door prejudiced the jury against him. Judge Dockery rejected the mistrial motion, but he instructed the jury to disregard Gilbert's testimony about the incident.

The judge also barred from consideration by the jury the testimony on Evans's request to Gilbert about taking the children.

James Edwards told his story of finding the bodies.

Wesley K. Rozema, a jail inmate, testified that Ward had told him while both were in the DuPage County Jail in 1997 that he "popped" Evans and her daughter, Samantha, but had nothing to do with Joshua's murder.

Myra Redding testified about hearing Ward threaten to kill Debra Evans when Redding visited in a Villa Park apartment Williams and Caffey were sharing in May 1995. Ward, Williams, Caffey, and another couple were present.

Redding said Ward came in angry and punched a hole in the wall because Evans would not let him see his son Jordan.

"Verne Ward stated he was done with Debbie," said Redding. "He wanted to kill her. He wanted it done then. He was tired of her." Redding admitted she used crack cocaine in 1995 and 1996, but she was not a user now.

Tina Martin told the jury of Ward's visit to her apartment shortly before 7:00 P.M. on the day of the murder and that he talked to Debbie on the phone, asking, "Is it mine or his?" (He was referring to the baby that Evans was expecting.)

Ward left on foot about 8:15 P.M., Martin said.

Two seventeen-year-old girls testified about Ward changing clothes in the apartment of a relative where the girls were on the evening of November 16, 1995. One girl said she noticed blood "on the top of his pants and his shirt." The other girl said she saw him go into the bathroom carrying a plastic grocery bag to change, but she had not noticed the blood.

One of the girls testified Ward then went outside, tossed the plastic bag of clothes from which he had changed into a gray car in which two or three people were waiting. One was a woman with "big, Afro-like" hair, the girl said.

While being cross-examined, the girl who had seen the blood admitted she never mentioned it in two interviews with police, nor in testimony before a grand jury, because she "didn't want to get involved."

The other girl testified she had heard her mother invite Ward to bring Debbie to Thanksgiving dinner at their home and that Ward had replied, "he wasn't going to be talking to Debbie anymore."

The state also called a witness, Jasper Harrington, who testified he had seen Ward with a two-speaker stereo that he apparently was trying to sell or trade on

Chicago's west side for drugs. The description of the stereo matched Samantha's missing portable stereo.

The final witness for the prosecution was Dwight Pruitt, who supported Scott's testimony about Joshua and the "burglars" he saw and later named before he was killed.

Under cross-examination Pruitt said, "I didn't hear him say they killed his mother and sister. He said Annette Williams was at the house. I took it to mean she was one of the burglars."

The state rested its case following Pruitt's appearance.

Several of Ward's relatives and friends took the witness chair to tell that he was with them at various periods of time on the evening and night of November 16 and into the early hours of November 17. Taken as a whole, the witnesses accounted for Ward's purported whereabouts during the crucial time period.

The defense also offered a witness to offset the testimony about Ward being seen in Chicago with a portable stereo. A nineteen-year-old woman friend of Ward's in Chicago testified a portable stereo or radio vanished from her car when Ward was using it two weeks before the murders—implying the stereo Ward had with him might have belonged to her.

TWENTY-NINE

The star of the legal showdown was on stage.

Laverne Ward, wearing a black suit, a white shirt, a tie, and highly polished shoes, took the witness stand on Monday, June 8, 1998.

Earl Washington got to the point immediately.

"Did you go to Debra Evans's house and commit a murder against Debra Evans?"

"No, I did not!" Ward said emphatically.

"Did you go to Debra Evans's house and commit murder against Samantha Evans?" Washington asked.

"No, I did not!"

"Did you help Annette Williams cut Debra Evans's body open and remove your son?"

"No, I did not! I wouldn't have never did nothing like that!" Ward exclaimed defiantly.

He told the jurors, looking directly at them and speaking calmly now, "I've been waiting for this for a long time—two and one half years."

Ward in his testimony denied that he changed from bloody clothing at a relative's house that fateful Thursday night. He said he was at the apartment, but he denied everything else that the two teenage girls had testified, calling them liars.

Ward admitted that he made a phone call to Debra Evans the evening of the murders from Tina Martin's house. He denied asking Evans in that conversation whether the baby "is his or mine?" He described the call as having been friendly, even to the point of Debra making him laugh.

Ward testified that the last time he had seen Debra was in July 1995, when she broke off their relationship. "She said I would never change. I would always be the same."

Ward was asked by his attorney to give an account of what he did and where he was on November 16, the day of the murders.

"It was like any other day, as far as I was concerned," Ward said. He denied that he was nervous-acting that day, as one witness had said. He denied meeting with Williams and Caffey at any time that day to plan the attacks, as the prosecutors accused him of doing.

Nor did he go to Chicago to sell or trade Samantha's portable, two-speaker stereo, he said.

He related that he and Debra had a friendly relationship and did not argue over his son Jordan. It was not until about 2:30 P.M. on Thursday, November 16, that he woke up in the apartment where he lived with his girlfriend and her three children, Ward related.

He recalled how he and his friend John Pettaway went to the house of his friend's brother and drank beer.

He said when they drove away, he saw Caffey and Williams in their car. He said he flagged them down and had a short talk about a basketball game Williams's son was playing in that evening at school.

That was the first time he had seen or talked to the couple for over a month, Ward said.

After drinking all day, Ward said, he tried to go home, but he found he was locked out and did not have his key. He went to the nearby home of Tina Martin and made some phone calls. He denied he had engaged in an angry phone conversation with Debra.

Leaving Martin's residence about 8:30 P.M. he walked to the home of an uncle in Wheaton. He arrived there about 9:00 P.M.

He said he changed clothes—not because there was blood on them—and left a short time later. He called the two girls "liars"—especially the one who testified there was blood on his clothing.

"Everybody in the neighborhood knows that," Ward said.

He returned to his girlfriend's place at 10:30 P.M. and went to sleep. He left about 3:00 A.M. to visit friends in Chicago, where he smoked marijuana and went back to Wheaton, he said. He had returned to Chicago about 7 A.M., on November 17, taking his girlfriend with him, he said.

Beginning his cross-examination of Ward, Prosecutor Kinsella moved to within three feet of the witness, standing directly in front of him.

He "barked" questions at Ward, as one newspaper reporter described it.

Ward kept his composure and stuck to his account of his activities.

Kinsella pressed hard for the witness to be specific about the time he was with people who were his alibis.

Ward's voice rose when he fired back at Kinsella: "Don't start me lying, because I don't know the exact times."

"Did you go back to Chicago for a reason?" Kinsella asked. "Was it to barter a stereo?"

"No," Ward answered.

"Was there something troubling you, sir?" Kinsella asked.

"No, I was with a female over there, and I'd told her I'd be back."

But as Kinsella questioned him on why he had taken his Wheaton girlfriend with him on that second trip to Chicago purportedly to see another woman, Ward was unable to give a reason.

During cross-examination by Kinsella, Ward could not explain how he recognized the gray Mercury Sable that Williams and Caffey were in when he stopped them. The car had been purchased only eight days earlier, and Ward had said he had not seen Williams and Caffey for over a month.

In closing, prosecutor Jeff Kendall stressed to the jury that "there was plenty of time to commit this crime, and it happened between two events: the defendant being at Tina Martin's home and the defendant arriving at his relative's house [where he changed clothes].

"These are not times that are marked on the face of a clock. It's not as if people are punching in and out of work. . . . You know the defendant had time to commit this crime, and you've seen it through the testimony of multiple witnesses and multiple facts. . . . Joshua Evans was an eyewitness to where the defendant was when the boy's mother and sister were murdered. You heard him speak to you through Patrice Scott and Dwight Pruitt in this courtroom."

After closing arguments by both sides, the jury retired to deliberate. It was no quick verdict this time. Williams's jury had returned with a guilty verdict in two hours.

The Ward jury was out for eleven hours before reaching its decision: guilty of three counts of murder, two counts of aggravated kidnapping, and one count of armed robbery.

As a court clerk read the verdict, Ward shook his head and placed his hand on his chin. He showed no emotion.

Attorney Earl Washington later told the news media that the case against Ward was "entirely circumstantial" and that the jury was swayed by emotion instead of the facts.

"Once those jurors were showed the horrific photos of those dead children, they could not restrain their tears," the defense lawyer said. "I think this dulled their ability to deal dispassionately with the facts and the evidence."

The Evans family met the verdict with tears and a sense of relief.

On the following Monday, the jury would decide

whether Ward would be given the death penalty—he had been ruled eligible for it—-or life in prison.

Before the closing arguments started on the penalty, Ward again was called to the stand by his attorney.

He asked the jury not to give him the death penalty.

"I'm not going to stop fighting until my innocence is proven," Ward said. "My goal is to fight on. I was young and dumb and made a lot of mistakes growing up on the street.

"I love kids. Children are the most precious things in the world. No way on God's green earth I would harm a child."

In his closing argument prosecutor Jeff Kendall told the jury: "Ward has earned the death penalty by his horrific actions. Ward made choices to commit his crimes. Debra, Sam, and Josh didn't get to make any choices. If this case doesn't require the death penalty, will there ever be a case?

"He butchered them. He slaughtered them."

Prosecutor Mike Wolfe said, "Any plea for mercy should offend you. Show Ward the same mercy he showed Debra, Samantha, and Joshua. He can't be allowed to spend the rest of his life frolicking in prison."

Attorney Washington, seeking to save his client's life, told the jury: "I hope and pray that there is one amongst you [to vote against the death penalty.] Vote for life and not for death."

Under the state law, if only one juror voted against the death penalty, the defendant's life would be spared.

Veteran attorney Washington believed that he had a good chance of getting a life imprisonment verdict instead of death.

He had argued hard that there was not one piece of physical evidence that tied Ward to the murders. He had been placed at the murder scene only by the testimony of Patrice Scott quoting the accusatory words of little Joshua. And Washington had hit hard at her as a "liar" when he said her testimony was too questionable to give Ward the death penalty.

Earl Washington's hopes were answered.

On June 22, after four hours of deliberation, the jury returned its verdict sparing Ward from death by lethal injection.

The divided jury had voted eight for the death penalty, four against.

Several jurors said later that the four jury members who voted against death were concerned about the absence of physical evidence connecting Ward to the murder scene in Addison.

One juror who favored the death penalty later explained: "Everyone agreed there was enough evidence to convict, but not for death." The verdict had come, the juror said, after "heated discussion, name-calling, and finger-pointing."

Debra Evans's sister, Wendy, told a reporter: "This is the one trial of the three that meant the most. I understand the system, but deep down it isn't fair for my sister. She didn't get to live the rest of her life, and he will."

Sam Evans thanked the jury, but the father admitted he was not happy with the verdict.

Attorney Washington said that after the verdict, Ward said to him, "Thank God."

DuPage County state attorney Joseph Birkett said, "Prosecutors and the Evans family must accept this level of justice. We believe we had enough evidence for the death penalty, but the jury made a different decision. It only takes one juror [to defeat a death verdict]."

On August 17, 1998, Judge Dockery formally sentenced Laverne Ward to three concurrent natural-life sentences for the three murders; fifteen years (concurrent with the life sentences) for aggravated kidnapping; and sixty years for armed robbery.

The judge made the armed robbery sentence consecutive to the other sentences, meaning Ward would not start serving the sixty years until his three natural-life sentences for the other crimes were served.

As Laura Pollastrini, spokeswoman for the DuPage County State Attorney's Office, explained to the news media:

"There's no parole. He'll never get out again."

Judge Dockery denied Ward's motion for a new trial, and Earl Washington announced he would appeal the verdict.

THIRTY

When the trial of Fedell Caffey began on Monday, October 26, 1998, he already had received one legal break. The court ruled as inadmissible in the Caffey trial the confession given by Annette Williams. It was the only "witness" evidence linking Caffey to the crimes except for Joshua's damning words of identification, which the jury would hear through Patrice Scott and Dwight Pruitt. And both of these witnesses, as in the trials of the other two defendants, would be under heavy defense attack of their credibility.

As for Caffey, his attorneys disclosed at the start that he would take the stand and deny any involvement in the bizarre and horrible crimes. He would testify that he was home baby-sitting with his girlfriend's children when Debra and her two older children were slaughtered, defense attorneys promised in their opening statements.

"Shocked" was how Caffey would describe—from the witness stand—his emotions when he first viewed the newborn infant that Williams brought home in her arms on the night of the triple homicides, the defense lawyers said.

Caffey, as he would tell it, had been baby-sitting Williams's children during the hours she was away apparently engaged in murder and atrocity. During the time that the murders and baby theft happened early that night, Fedell was playing a video game with one of Williams's daughters, said his attorneys.

He had nothing to do with the butchery on North Swift Road in Addison, the defense declared.

Defense attorneys declared in their opening remarks that Caffey was a "dupe, a fall guy"—himself an innocent victim of the murderous plot hatched and carried out by Annette Williams and her cousin Laverne Ward. Caffey was "surprised" when he first saw Williams with the baby, said the defense.

For the third time before a jury, prosecutors Kinsella, Kendall, and Wolfe told a now-familiar story in their opening statements. The motive for the murders and looting of Debra Evans's womb was to get a light-skinned baby boy, which Williams believed was necessary to keep her boyfriend, Caffey, said the state lawyers.

Williams could not produce any baby herself, for she had had a tubal ligation after her last child was born.

Caffey was involved fully in the womb robbery murders and kidnappings, the prosecution told the jury.

Prosecutor Wolfe stressed, "They were caught with the proceeds of, and the motive, for these horrific crimes." He referred to the arrest of Annette Williams and Fedell Caffey as the couple returned to their Schaumburg town house—Williams carrying the baby in her arms and Caffey holding a baby car seat and wearing a bloodstained jacket taken from the murder scene.

Wolfe said that the baby was no surprise to Caffey. The assistant state attorney pointed out that Caffey had told a friend that very night and before the murders, "We are going to have the baby tonight."

But defense attorney Paul DeLuca told the jury of six women and six men: "A terrible crime did occur at Debra Evans's apartment in Addison. Fedell Caffey was not there."

He agreed partially with the state attorneys' contention that Williams faked a pregnancy and then conspired with others to kill Evans and take her baby so that Caffey would believe she had borne him a child.

"This was a plan to dupe him, to cement and seal this relationship with him," said DeLuca. He called Caffey "a fool, a fall guy, the set-up guy, a sucker in this case. [But] the real perpetrators of this terrible crime are not in the court today."

DeLuca declared that it was Williams who had the motive to steal the baby because she was "crazy jealous" about Caffey previously having a daughter with another girlfriend.

The defense attorney related that Williams gorged on food to gain weight for the role she had assumed as an expectant mother. The attorney said Williams told everyone she was pregnant and attended a baby shower for herself.

After she had told Caffey different dates for the baby's arrival, Caffey made fun of her, said the lawyer. As her designated "due" dates came and went with no birth, Caffey said he did not believe her pregnancy claims.

On the night of the murders, Caffey was at home trying to locate Williams by telephone, DeLuca said.

Taking the stand as a state witness, Tina Martin, Annette's sister, testified that Caffey had claimed to be the father of the baby Williams was expecting and had attended a baby shower for her. (Caffey later said he attended the shower and bought Annette a present at her request.)

Martin was asked in cross-examination if she had received a phone call from Caffey at 1:30 A.M. on November 17, 1995, several hours after the murders, in which he said he was looking for Williams. Replying yes, Martin said Caffey had asked her to page Williams to let her know he was looking for her.

Kasandra Turner, a female friend of Williams's, dealt another blow to the defense claim that Caffey knew nothing about the newborn baby until Williams came home with it in her arms. The witness testified that Caffey phoned her home about 6 P.M. on Thursday, November 16, 1995—which would have been before the killings—to tell her he would soon be a father.

Turner quoted Caffey as saying, "Guess what? We're going to have the baby." To which Turner said she replied, "Call me and let me know when you have it."

The next day, Turner said, she heard from friends that Williams's and Caffey's baby had been born. The woman said she paged Williams, but it was Caffey who returned the page.

Turner said she told Caffey she had heard their baby had been born.

Caffey had answered, "Yeah, we had a boy," the woman recalled.

She asked Caffey who the baby looked like, and he said, "I don't know. I know one thing, though. He's real light-skinned."

She testified she went to the Schaumburg town house the next night to see the baby, but she was prohibited from entering by armed police officers who surrounded the residence.

The state's case, for the most part, was a repetition of the other two trials, including Pruitt and Scott. The couple testified again about Joshua's telling them that the apartment burglars who "cut his mommy and sister" were Williams, Caffey, and Ward.

The defense cross-exam of Scott centered on why she had not called the police or "done something" to help Joshua after he first made his accusations on the early morning he was brought by Williams to the apartment shared by Scott and Pruitt. Again, Scott told of her intense fear for her baby's life and her own, afraid to do anything until she could safely get away from the killers.

Launching its case, the defense called a woman who testified to going to the Schaumburg town house to buy crack cocaine from Caffey on the night of November 16.

She said it was 6:30 or 7:00 P.M. when she visited the town house. She said she did not see Williams, but she was there only a few minutes to make the drug buy from Caffey.

* * *

Fedell Caffey spoke quietly and in an unchanging tone of voice as he testified about the events of November 16, 1995.

He said that Annette Williams left their town house about 7:00 P.M., ostensibly to attend a class.

About 2:30 A.M. his girlfriend arrived home with a newborn baby in her arms, he related. She was accompanied by her friend Betty Larson, and when he met them at the door, Larson exclaimed, "Surprise! Meet Fedell Caffey Jr.!"

Caffey recalled he was skeptical. "It's just shocking. Where would they get a baby at two-thirty in the morning? The baby's umbilical cord was bleeding. That was what was persuading me to believe that this goofy story they were telling me was true."

According to Caffey, he had been told by Larson that Williams was visiting in Larson's home when she began having the baby, and Larson had taken her to the Du-Page County Hospital, where the infant was delivered.

Williams said that she left the hospital after the baby was born because she did not have insurance. Caffey claimed he had been at home all the time Williams was gone. He said he played video games with one of her daughters and sold crack to two customers.

The defendant testified he became worried about 1:30 A.M. when Williams was not back, and that is why he called Tina Martin. He said he called from a nearby convenience store's pay phone.

A clerk at the store had testified for the state earlier that Annette Williams was with Caffey when he made the phone call. Caffey said he was alone when he called and that the call made when Williams was with him was later that morning, when he and Annette went back to the store to buy some baby wipes.

Caffey admitted that he was a crack cocaine dealer, but he said, "I would never kill a child."

Caffey testified he had never met the Evans children and had no reason to kill them. But under a probing cross-examination, Caffey could give no answer as to why a white electric cord with Joshua's blood on it was found in Caffey's garage; or why a sheet stained with the boy's blood found blocks from the boy's body and that matched a fitted sheet officers located in the town house; or why Joshua's body was dumped in an area where Caffey once lived and admittedly was familiar with.

Caffey himself, while testifying, admitted he had visited that alley at least twenty times during the period he lived in that part of Maywood.

THIRTY-ONE

What was Fedell Caffey: a cold-blooded killer of women and children, or the fall guy in a murderous plot?

That was the big question before the jury.

As far as Caffey's testimony that he was "duped" was concerned, prosecutor Jeff Kendall told the jury that "it was a pack of lies."

Kendall went down the list of testimony and evidence that tied the drug-dealing defendant to the gruesome murders; the butchering of Debra Evans to get her baby, and the kidnappings of the baby and Joshua, whom Caffey ultimately stabbed to death.

Said Kendall: Caffey had on James Edwards's stolen and bloodstained college jacket when arrested; he was carrying a baby car seat; the knife that killed Joshua was found in the dishwasher in Caffey and Williams's town house; the bloody sheet used to wrap the stabbed Joshua, which was found along a street not far from his dumped body, matched a fitted sheet discovered in Caffey's home; the white cable cord with a spot of Joshua's blood on it was recovered from the town house garage; and Joshua's blood was found in the back of the gray Mercury Sable owned by Caffey and Williams.

Together, it was an inventory of guilt. Kendall sketched a diagram depicting the string of unrelated witnesses who testified against Caffey in the trial.

"He was not set up. He was not duped," Kendall declared. "The crack kingpin didn't get the wool pulled over his eyes."

Kendall referred to the bizarre murder plot as "Caffey's little lie passing off Eli as Fedell Caffey Jr. to the rest of the world."

The defense lawyers agreed with prosecutors when they argued that Williams attempted to keep Caffey's love by bringing him the kind of baby he wanted: a light-skinned boy. The only difference from the state's theory: Caffey was not with her when it all happened.

The prosecution referred to Caffey as "a cold-blooded murderer of defenseless women and children."

Defense attorneys Dan Cunningham and Paul DeLuca lashed out at Patrice Scott, dwelling on why she did not call the police or do something to save Joshua's life after he first told of Williams, Ward, and Caffey breaking into the Addison apartment, killing the mother and daughter, and ripping the baby from her womb.

The defense questioned her credibility and advanced their theory of her involvement in the murder of Joshua. Caffey simply was being framed by Williams, Scott, and Ward, the defense lawyers declared.

Cunningham asked the jury in closing arguments, "Why would . . . Fedell Caffey kill three people to have and raise Verne Ward's child? Why would he want Ward's child at all? There is no reason."

The jury deliberated for five and a half hours before returning to the courtroom with its verdict, finding Caffey guilty of all the charges against him.

Caffey showed no reaction to the verdict. He had shown none throughout the trial.

Wheaton Daily Herald reporter Robert McCoppin reported that after Caffey was found guilty, he believed it would not help him for the defense to bring out his personal childhood background.

But the man who had remained stoic during the gruesome testimony of the trial, broke into tears when his attorneys told the jury he had been raised without a father, and his mother and grandmother were schizophrenic. All of this had a bearing on his life of crime, said the defense.

Caffey was a member of the Boy Scouts, played basketball in school, and graduated from high school in Maywood. But he joined a gang and began pushing crack cocaine, the jury was told.

He reportedly had quit a legitimate job because he could make as much as $1,000 or more a week dealing drugs.

The jury was out one hour and forty minutes and then returned with a verdict of death for Caffey.

Ironically, the verdict came on November 17, 1998— exactly three years to the day after Joshua Evans was slain and left in the alley in Caffey's hometown.

The defense attorneys said they would appeal the conviction because the jury should have heard other witnesses who would have confirmed Caffey's story but who refused to testify because they were awaiting trial on indictments charging them with having "covered up the crime." The lawyers apparently were referring to the man and two women involved in obtaining and later disposing of the murder gun and of obstructing justice.

Prosecutors Kinsella, Kendall, and Wolfe had spent twenty weeks in court on the Evans case in 1998.

Following the verdict, Kinsella said: "All of us have a sense of relief having gone through this long ordeal over this year. We are trying to seek justice for Debbie and her children, so it's a great motivator."

On January 22, 1999, Fedell Caffey appeared before Judge Peter Dockery for formal sentencing.

In the few words that he spoke to the judge before the sentence was pronounced, Caffey continued to claim he was not guilty of the vicious crimes.

He said, "How I got messed up in this, I do not know. No matter how many times a judge or jury convicts me of this, I will never be guilty of that murder. It's not true."

Judge Dockery formally sentenced Caffey to death by lethal injection, setting his execution for March 26, 1999. But he suspended the imposition of the death sentence while it was automatically appealed to the Illinois Supreme Court.

Meanwhile, Prosecutor Wolfe spoke words of praise for the "passionate, honest, and thorough work" of the fifteen law enforcement agencies that worked on the

Evans murder investigation. He cited the outstanding investigative work of Detectives Mark Van Stedum and Michael Simo of the Addison Police Department, who led the lengthy and around-the-clock investigation.

The defense attorneys pointed to eighty-five points in which they claimed Caffey's case had been handled improperly and which they said would be the basis of subsequent appeals.

In the next few months, the three suspects under indictment on charges of furnishing the gun used in Debra Evans's murder and later disposing of it, and obstructing justice, were tried and received jail sentences.

In August 1999, Betty Larson pleaded guilty to charges of "unlawful use of a weapon and obstruction of justice."

She said, "There is no excuse for what I did. I live with this every single day."

She admitted that she gave Annette Williams a .25-caliber handgun. But she said that Williams had told her she was using the gun for protection in a drug deal.

She denied knowing that the gun would be used for the murder of Debra Evans.

She admitted that she and Alice Pirtle threw the weapon into Herrick Lake near Wheaton. She later led officers to the spot.

During the hearing Larson said that since the gun episode she had been "straightening out" her life and had stayed off drugs and alcohol.

DuPage County Circuit judge George Banals sentenced Larson to two years' probation, plus 180 days in county jail and also fifty hours of public service. The judge agreed that she would be allowed to work during the day on her job as a truck driver.

Pirtle received a sentence of two years on probation; she also was sentenced to work eight hours a day for ten days on Sheriff's Department work assignments such as picking up garbage and other similar jobs.

Maurice Wuertz was sentenced to two years' probation and ten days in county jail.

There was one big unanswered question of the otherwise successful murder investigation: Who was the unknown fourth "burglar" that Joshua Evans later remembered as "Boo Boo" or "Bo"?

The only person the detectives could find with the nickname of "Bo," whom Joshua would have known by sight if he saw him, was a distant relative of Laverne Ward's: Bo Carlton.

The investigators questioned Carlton at length. Carlton gave them the name of a witness who he said could verify that Carlton was elsewhere when the murders took place that Thursday, November 16, 1995, in the North Swift apartment.

The witness backed Carlton's alibi, which would remain unshaken. The sleuths turned up no evidence that would link Carlton to the slayings.

There was another suspect that the homicide men checked. The man, Ware Upshaw, who was called "Pig," was a known associate of the convicted killers. But when he was questioned, he also had an alibi. He

said he had been at work at a warehouse on the night
of the murders. When the detectives examined his time
cards at the warehouse, they found one dated November
16 that showed he was working during the crucial
hours. But there was one unusual thing about his card
for that night. The time of his shift was handwritten,
not machine-printed like all of the others.

The handwritten time card never was explained. The
handwriting never was linked to Upshaw or any of the
workers or supervisors in the large warehouse.

The detectives were left with nothing to disprove the
suspect's claim that he was at work. After being questioned, Upshaw hired a lawyer. And within a short time,
he left town for Los Angeles, California.

"If we ever get evidence against a fourth person, he
will be charged and tried," said ASA John Kinsella.

The detectives and the prosecutors are inclined to
believe Joshua's story that a fourth "burglar" was in
the apartment and that the boy apparently knew him by
sight and a nickname. That four persons were involved
was further bolstered by the woman resident of the
apartment complex who had seen four people, three
men and a woman, talking in the parking lot that Thursday night. Two of the men matched the general descriptions of Ward and Caffey, and the third man was
"shorter" than either of the others. The woman was
believed by the officers to have been Williams.

There also was the testimony of the two teenage girls
who recalled seeing Ward coming to the apartment in
bloodstained clothes and "three or four" other persons
waiting outside in the gray car—one of which was a
woman with a big "Afro-style" hairdo. One of the girls

said she had seen two men and a woman in the car while Ward was inside changing clothes.

As for Joshua's account to Patrice Scott that "four burglars came in the window," the investigators speculate that Joshua may have awakened just as the intruders passed in front of, or were standing by, the window in his bedroom. And a breeze may have stirred the curtain, lending to the illusion that they had come through the window.

There was no evidence that forced entry had been made through that window located about ten feet above ground level. Investigators think the killers were admitted voluntarily by Debra Evans.

The window was raised slightly for ventilation, as it was regularly, the detectives learned. The double-pane window was removed and examined thoroughly, but no fingerprints other than the apartment occupants' were on it.

Oddly enough, a boot print was found between the two panes of glass and had been there apparently ever since the window was installed. Investigators speculated the boot print was that of a worker who accidentally walked on one of the panes as it lay on the ground before the glass was put in the window.

To this day, the identity of the "fourth" burglar is unknown.

EPILOGUE

On August 12, 1999, DuPage County state attorney Joseph Birkett announced that the four attorneys who were prosecutors in the trials of all three defendants in the Debra Evans murder had received a prestigious national award for their roles in the lengthy case.

The Association of Government Attorneys in Capital Litigation gave the award to John Kinsella, first assistant state attorney; Michael Wolfe, criminal prosecutions bureau chief, felony division; Jeffrey Kendall, criminal prosecutions bureau deputy chief; and Elizabeth Ekl, assistant state attorney.

Also honored was Colin Simpson of the Cook County State's Attorney's Office for his role in the investigation of the case.

The honor bestowed on the attorneys was the Regional Vice President's Award for Region II's 1998–99 Trial Advocacy Award.

The award usually is given to only one attorney in each region throughout the nation, but all of the Evans case prosecutors were nominated and all four received the award.

The Association of Government Attorneys in Capital Litigation is a national organization of prosecutors at both trial and appellate level who are involved in the prosecution of death penalty cases.

Region II comprises those states within the Midwest that have the death penalty.

State Attorney Birkett praised the recipients of the award:

"I am extremely proud of John, Mike, Jeff, and Beth for the outstanding job they did in the prosecution of these heinous murders. Their devotion to this case and their commitment to the administration of justice should be a model for all prosecutors to follow. This award from our peers throughout the nation is appreciated by not only the four prosecutors who tried the cases, but by all of the staff members of the DuPage County State Attorney's Office."

In March 2000 the voluminous Evans file had been stored in the courthouse basement for months.

Kinsella, Kendall, Wolfe, and Ekl were back to ordinary work schedules, which always keeps them busy.

Annette Williams was confined on death row in the Dwight Correctional Center at Dwight, Illinois. Some might wonder if the name of the prison reminded Williams of one of the key witnesses responsible for her being there: Dwight Pruitt, who helped to carry Joshua Evans's words about the identity of his mother and sister's killers into the courtroom and before a jury—literally the testimony of a tough little kid from the grave.

Laverne Ward was an inmate at the Joliet Correctional Center in Joliet, Illinois.

Fedell Caffey was on death row in the Menard Correctional Center at Menard, Illinois.

Scott Gilbert, the father of Samantha Evans, was operating Sam's Martial Arts School for the Korean martial art of Tae Kwon Do, in Wheaton, Illinois. Gilbert named the school after his slain daughter.

"I wanted to make a difference, if there was any way I could, in the protection of especially children, that they might be able to better defend themselves from such attacks as took the life of my Samantha," Gilbert said.

He has students ranging in age from five to fifty-three. The school has classes at night about three times a week. During the day Gilbert works as a garage-door hanger, an occupation he has been in for years.

Gilbert said his life is slowly returning to normal, but he still has nightmares about the savage murders. For over two years, his deep depression over the untimely and brutal deaths of his daughter, her mother, and her brother threatened his marriage, rendering him almost unable to cope.

But in 2000 he was on his way back from the hellish nightmare that devastated his life in November 1995.

He said the terrible dreams are less frequent now.

He and his wife have two daughters, two and five years old. The little girls, too, will learn martial arts.

Elijah Evans, who was a few months over four years old in 2000, and his older brother Jordan, six years old, were under the care of their grandfather, Sam Evans, at last report.

The brothers were very close from the beginning, relatives said, and the horrors that traumatized their young lives that terrifying November 16, 1995, have continued to fade into the past. Jordan is ultra-protective of his little brother, but the young brothers have been assured that all the "bad guys," as Jordan called them, will never be harming anyone else.

Seemingly, the nighttime fears that haunted the boys have vanished mostly through their quiet rural existence, where loving care, including church attendance, is a part of their lives.

Jordan walks with his arm around the shoulders of his brother and displays an attitude of watching over him, reassuring him.

The Addison Police Department's investigative unit and the DuPage County State Attorney's Office are working mostly regular shifts nowadays. But memories remain strong with the homicide detectives and the prosecutors in the Evans case. They hope nothing like it will ever happen again.

Ordinary days envelop the DuPage County Court Facility. The premises around the court building reflect a pastoral kind of quietness and peace.

The ducks and other waterfowl glide smoothly over the nearby lake, until a sudden opportunity for food sends them flailing into the air in a loud whir of wings.

It is a peaceful setting far removed from the nightmarish horror of grisly testimony and nerve-grinding legal wars that prevailed in that large criminal courtroom on the fourth floor—drawing many spectators and a large corps of news media people whose newspaper and television and radio reports went around the world.

Now, quietness prevails most of the time.

Yet, so many good people will be so terribly haunted the rest of their lives.

ACKNOWLEDGMENTS

I appreciate so much the excellent cooperation and courtesies I received during my research for this book from the DuPage County (Illinois) Office of the State Attorney, Joseph E. Birkett, and his exceptional staff of felony prosecutors.

John Kinsella, first assistant state's attorney; and Jeffrey Kendall, Michael Wolfe, and Elizabeth Ekl, assistant state attorneys, all were especially helpful in directing me to necessary court documents and trial transcripts and giving me an insight into the job they did in the preparation and prosecution of this high-priority case that claimed most of their regular, and many overtime, hours from 1995 through 1998.

I also want to thank the efficient and courteous secretarial and reception staff of the office for guiding me where I needed to go and helping me find my way out.

The professional job the prosecutors and their staffs did on the Debra Evans murder case has to rank as one of the best I ever encountered in my many years of covering criminal courts and the police beat and following the true-crime book trail.

SA Birkett and his prosecutors are people dedicated to their goal of justice.

I also want to thank Detective Mark Van Stedum and the other homicide investigators of the Addison Police Department who cooperated with me to the extent they were allowed in a case still in the appeal process.

They are dedicated men and women who know their job and do it so well.

I am grateful for the help I received from Ms. Laura M. Pollastrini, who is public information and special projects manager for the DuPage County State Attorney's Office.

Although I do not know their names, I thank the security people who every day during my visits to the Judicial Facility Office in Wheaton, Illinois, patiently endured and sorted through the strange odds and ends I carry on my person and in a briefcase.

The DuPage County seat of Wheaton, Illinois, is a nice town to visit. The folks are courteous and helpful. If I didn't like Texas so much, I might move there.

I'm especially grateful to the personnel at Chicago Midway Airport, who spotted my briefcase I left beside a soft-drink machine and turned it into the American Airline ticket counter attendants, who alerted me that the briefcase was there.

The briefcase contained all of the audiotapes and trial transcript copies and photographs and other material gathered in the research of this book.

Had I lost it, I would have run screaming over the horizon, never to be seen again, and this book would not have been written.

I thank my wife, Nina, who patiently supports me in all of my shortcomings and moments of near madness, in addition to her being an adept researcher and expert copy editor.

As always, too, I thank my book editor Karen Haas and editor-in-chief Paul Dinas for their patience and endurance.

Bill G. Cox
March 9, 2000

Bill Cox passed away unexpectedly in May 2000. He had an eye for finding good stories, a knack for careful research, and a dedication to his profession. We will miss him.

Kensington Publishing